*The Modern Age
and the
Recovery of Ancient Wisdom*

The Modern Age and the Recovery of Ancient Wisdom

A Reconsideration of
Historical Consciousness, 1450–1650

Stephen A. McKnight

University of Missouri Press

Columbia and London

Copyright © 1991 by
The Curators of the University of Missouri
University of Missouri Press, Columbia, Missouri 65201
Printed and bound in the United States of America
All rights reserved
5 4 3 2 1   95 94 93 92 91

Library of Congress Cataloging-in-Publication Data

McKnight, Stephen A., 1944–
　The modern age and the recovery of ancient wisdom : a reconsideration of historical consciousness, 1450–1650 / Stephen A. McKnight.
　　p.　cm.
　Includes bibliographical references and index.
　ISBN 0-8262-0781-2 (alk. paper)
　1. Renaissance. 2. Europe—Intellectual life—16th century.
3. Europe—Intellectual life—17th century. I. Title.
CB367.M35　1991
940.2'1—dc20　　　　　　　　　　　　　　　　　　　　　　　91-12866
　　　　　　　　　　　　　　　　　　　　　　　　　　　　　　　CIP

∞™ This paper meets the minimum requirements of the American National Standard for Permanence of Paper for Printed Library Materials, Z39.48, 1984.

Designer: Rhonda Gibson
Typesetter: Connell-Zeko Type & Graphics
Printer: Thomson-Shore, Inc.
Binder: Thomson-Shore, Inc.
Typeface: Sabon

For my parents, with love and gratitude.

Contents

Acknowledgments   ix

Introduction   1

1. Blumenberg and Modernity   6
2. The Renaissance Revival of the *Prisca Theologia*   27
3. Ficino and the *Prisca Theologia* Tradition   42
4. Christian and Neoplatonic Themes in Renaissance Art   60
5. The Hermetic *Paideia* in Botticelli's Art   91
6. The *Prisca Theologia* and the Modern Age   109
7. Francis Bacon: Ancient Wisdom and Utopian Reform   127

Conclusion   143

Bibliography   145

Index   157

Acknowledgments

I gratefully acknowledge permission from the following to quote from their publications: MIT Press for Hans Blumenberg, *The Legitimacy of the Modern Age,* translated by Robert M. Wallace; Shoe String Press for Giordano Bruno, *The Ash Wednesday Supper,* edited and translated by Edward A. Gosselin and Lawrence S. Lerner; Warburg and Courtauld Institutes and Charles Dempsey for his "'Mercurius Ver': The Sources of Botticelli's 'Primavera'"; Mouton de Gruyter for Robert Segal, *The Poimandres as Myth;* Charles Trinkaus for *In Our Image and Likeness;* University of Chicago Press and Routledge for Frances Yates, *Giordano Bruno and the Hermetic Tradition;* Center for Medieval and Early Renaissance Studies for *Marsilio Ficino: Three Books on Life: A Critical Edition and Translation with Introduction and Notes,* edited by Carol V. Kaske and John R. Clark.

All photographs of art in the text appear courtesy of Alinari/Art Resource, New York. I also wish to express my gratitude to the Earhart Foundation for a 1989 summer grant that allowed me to complete the research and writing of chapter 7.

Finally, I wish to thank Jay Malone for research assistance and my wife, Becky, for typing and editorial assistance.

*The Modern Age
and the
Recovery of Ancient Wisdom*

Introduction

The purpose of this study is to open a different perspective on the origins and development of a distinctly modern mode of historical construction and interpretation. This conception is characterized by its emphasis on an epochal break with the past that is frequently symbolized as an advance from darkness to light. This epochal leap is attributed to an epistemological breakthrough that transforms modern man into the active shaper of his fate by providing a means of controlling nature and perfecting society. Studies of this optimistic, progressivist construction usually trace it to the Enlightenment emphasis on the power of science and technology to transform the human condition by dispelling the ignorance and error of traditional metaphysics and religion.

This study departs from such an approach by showing that an optimistic, progressivist construction appeared much earlier than the eighteenth century and that a key influence on its formation was a tradition of occult philosophy and esoteric religion that was revived as part of the Renaissance recovery of ancient learning. This tradition included Hermeticism, Cabala, alchemy, and astral magic. Since the nineteenth century, these materials have frequently been referred to as "pseudo-science": false, primitive efforts at understanding the workings of nature. In the early modern period, however, many philosophers and theologians regarded these materials as part of a *prisca theologia* (Ancient Wisdom), a pristine revelation by God to the great wisemen of the Ancient Near East and Mediterranean. When first recovered by Ficino and the Neoplatonists, this material was believed to be the key to establishing a universal theology that could reconcile Christian belief with the essential core of ancient philosophy and religion.

To demonstrate that this *prisca theologia* tradition does indeed influence the modern progressivist concept of history requires that two lines of analysis be developed. First, it is necessary to demonstrate formal parallels between the Ancient Wisdom tradition and the characteristic features of modern epochal consciousness. This will be done through a detailed analysis of Ancient Wisdom texts that express the same epochal juxtaposition of an advance from darkness to light and attribute the advance to the discovery of knowledge that allows man to control nature and perfect society. Having established these parallels, it will then be necessary to demonstrate that this conception entered the mainstream of early modern thought and influenced the metaphysical and historical views of seminal figures of the modern age. As the study's subtitle indicates, the focus will be the span from 1450 until 1650, the period from the introduction of this tradition by Ficino and the Platonic Academy until its use in Francis Bacon's utopian program of political instauration through science.

Development of this line of analysis also imposes an obligation to relate the materials and interpretation offered here to current trends in the study of the origins and character of modernity. For this purpose, I have chosen to develop a detailed comparison with Hans Blumenberg's well-known and highly influential work *The Legitimacy of the Modern Age*. Several factors led to the choice of this work. Blumenberg's analysis focuses on the same basic features of modernity and the same general time period—the transition phase from the late medieval to the early modern period. Blumenberg also identifies the characteristic features of the modern age with its emphasis on progress and on human self-determination or "self-assertion," and he contends that the source of modern self-assertion is an epistemological transformation that purports to equip man with the ability to control nature and thereby to be able to perfect society. In tracing the origins of this epistemological shift, Blumenberg explores the "epochal threshold" linking the late phases of medieval theology to the early stages of modern philosophy. According to Blumenberg, modern historical consciousness takes shape during this epochal shift; consequently, developments in the eighteenth and nineteenth centuries cannot be properly understood apart from this formative stage.

These similarities also establish a context that allows fundamental differences to be brought into sharp focus. Two of the most important should be noted briefly here. The first has to do with the relation of Christian theology to modern self-assertion. Blumenberg maintains that human self-assertion in the modern age is the logical and necessary result of the exhaustion of medieval theology. According to his interpretation, the contradictory views of Scholasticism and Nominalism are the result of the early Church's ambiguous attitude toward the world. From the outset, the church fathers were confronted with a tradition that affirmed an omnipotent Creator, yet asserted that a Savior was needed to rescue man from life in the world. Blumenberg believed that the problem of theodicy—reconciling God's omnipotence with pervasive evil—forced an increasing emphasis on God's separation from the creation and from direct involvement in human affairs. When God becomes Nominalism's *deus absconditus,* the world loses its rational base and man is left to find whatever meaning and purpose he can through his own efforts. It is this context, Blumenberg contends, that leads to the modern project of self-affirmation and self-assertion.

The argument advanced here moves in a fundamentally different direction. Rather than trace a growing emphasis on dualism and God's radical transcendence, this study shows the important role played by an immanentist theological tradition that gains prominence during the Renaissance. This immanentist tradition affirms the goodness of the world and the dignity of man as a cocreator with God. A basic difference between this study and Blumenberg's, therefore, is in the understanding of the relation of theology to human self-assertion. Blumenberg stresses a radical dualism in late medieval thought that necessitates human self-assertion; this study concentrates on the affinities between Renaissance immanentism and modern self-assertion.

A second basic contrast with Blumenberg's work arises from the sources that challenged orthodox thought and resulted in the modern break with traditional theology and philosophy. For Blumenberg, Christianity never overcame the challenge of Gnostic dualism. Although Augustine and the early fathers succeeded in dealing with the immediate threat of the heretical sect, the solution was ultimately unsatisfactory and led to a second Gnostic revolt in the form of Nominalism. The argument presented here maintains that the ancient tradition that has to be taken into account is not Gnostic dualism but the immanentist strands of the *prisca theologia*. Analysis will show that this tradition had close parallels with the theological traditions of the Florentine Renaissance. Subsequently, however, it became disassociated from orthodox thought and tied to science and programs of utopian reform.

This thesis is developed over seven chapters. The first introduces the basic themes and issues of the study through a detailed examination of Blumenberg's *The Legitimacy of the Modern Age*. This analysis follows the course briefly described above. It first develops Blumenberg's criticisms of conventional views of modernity, then describes his own approach, and finally demonstrates how the *prisca theologia* has a fundamental bearing on the theoretical and historiographical issues he introduces. The second chapter then examines the Ancient Wisdom materials themselves. Particular attention is given to the immanentist themes found in the Hermetic teachings. This strand of the *prisca theologia* has been selected because of its influence on Ficino and other leading figures of the fifteenth and sixteenth centuries. The purpose of this analysis is to demonstrate that these texts have the following parallels with modern epochal views: they describe the present as the beginning of a new age of light; they identify the coming of the new age with the discovery of knowledge; and they maintain that this newly acquired knowledge transforms man into a terrestrial god capable of dominating nature and creating a utopian existence.

The third chapter examines two of Ficino's most important works, the *Theologia Platonica* and *De vita triplici*, to show the influence of Hermetic themes. This analysis focuses on Ficino's new understanding of man as a terrestrial god and shows how his immanentist linking of the micro- and macrocosms introduced the use of astral magic to overcome fate. The fourth and fifth chapters develop more fully the religious context in which the *prisca theologia* is introduced. As already noted, the intent is to demonstrate that an important strand of orthodox religion had a strong "incarnational" emphasis and that it was, therefore, far more compatible and receptive to the immanentism of the *prisca theologia* than a radically dualistic theology would have been. In order to establish that these views were part of the mainstream of Renaissance religion, the analysis shows their abiding presence in the iconography of some of the most important religious art of the Renaissance. Chapter 4 focuses on Giotto's frescoes at the Scrovegni Chapel in Padua as a prime example of Christian incarnational theology. The intent is to relate the religious themes in these paintings to the Renaissance and early modern celebration of human dignity, individuality, and the natural world. This chapter also examines the complex blending of Christian and Neoplatonic imagery in Michelangelo's Medici Chapel in Florence with the intention of showing the basic compatibility of Renaissance Christian thought with elements of the *prisca theologia* tradition that Ficino and the Platonic Academy introduced into the intellectual and political circles in Italy.

The fifth chapter continues the investigation of Neoplatonic and Hermetic themes and images by examining three paintings of Botticelli, *Minerva and the Centaur*, *The Birth of Venus*, and *La Primavera*. This analysis provides further evidence of the influence of those views of man, nature, and salvation through knowledge that are embodied in the Ancient Wisdom. The sixth chapter examines the mounting tension between orthodox Christian views and the *prisca theologia* in the sixteenth and seventeenth centuries, revealing that the truth of the *prisca theologia* was increasingly juxtaposed to the disorder and confusion of Christian thought. Attention to the writings of Agrippa, Bruno, and Campanella delineates an emerging tradition that increasingly identified Christian thought with ignorance and darkness while viewing the *prisca theologia* as the source of truth and light. In this crucial stage, the *prisca theologia* came to serve as the means of restoring man's true nature as a *magus*; when this restoration is made, man is able to create a paradise on earth.

Introduction

At this point, the discussion moves to the relation between the revival of the Ancient Wisdom and the emergence of the new science. Bruno and Campanella both regard the work of Copernicus and Galileo as the beginning of the new age, and Bruno even describes Copernicus as a John the Baptist who prepares the way for his own messianic appearance.

The seventh chapter addresses Francis Bacon's vision of a great instauration through knowledge, relating Bacon's emphasis on the soteriological role of science to utopian themes in the Ancient Wisdom tradition. Bacon has, of course, been heralded as a patriarch of science and modernity since the Enlightenment. A reassessment of his work in relation to the *prisca theologia* can therefore demonstrate how conventional assumptions must be reexamined. Bacon also receives detailed treatment because he plays a prominent role in Blumenberg's analysis of self-assertion. Analysis of Bacon's writings therefore provides a case study of fundamental similarities and differences between this study and Blumenberg's. The Conclusion draws together the main lines of the analysis and underscores its implications for the study of modernity and modern historical consciousness.

A brief word must be said about the general format and perspective taken here. The effort to reach scholars from several disciplines who are interested in the analysis of modernity has had two effects on the approach and format. First, I have attempted to concentrate as much as possible on basic theoretical and historiographical issues affected by the *prisca theologia* tradition. To do so, I have had to offer a relatively concise argument and direct my analysis toward major figures known to scholars in several fields. The treatment I am able to give major themes and thinkers can only suggest the more detailed study that should be undertaken. The second effect on format is that I have attempted to provide references in the footnotes and Bibliography that will be useful to an interdisciplinary audience. Specialists in various fields can rightly criticize omissions. My intent, however, is not to be exhaustive, but to select representative works that either indicate the current state of debate or contain bibliographies that will lead more deeply into the issues. In an effort to reach a broad audience, I have also used existing translations of primary sources or I have paraphrased or translated them myself. Scholars who want to look at the primary sources in the original languages will find detailed references to the principal critical editions in the notes and Bibliography. Moreover, where it is germane to my analysis, I offer my own emendations to the translations I am using or point to key symbolizations that might not be as obvious in the translation as they need to be.

1. Blumenberg and Modernity

For the last twenty-five years Hans Blumenberg has been engaged in a reassessment of the intellectual and cultural developments at the core of the epochal shift from the medieval to the modern age.[1] According to Blumenberg, a fundamental shift in approach and perspective was necessary in order to move beyond the errors and limitations of theoretical and historiographical interpretations, which had become mired down in the debate over secularization. His diagnosis of the flaws in the concept of secularization and his subsequent reinterpretation of the origins of modernity required Blumenberg to reconstruct the two epochal transitions in European history and to introduce new theoretical categories to mark these epochal shifts. This chapter will examine Blumenberg's best-known and most-influential work, *The Legitimacy of the Modern Age,* and develop a comparison with the analysis offered here. For the present purpose the most important components of Blumenberg's work are (1) his criticism of the flaws in the concept of secularization, (2) his contention that the origins of modern historical consciousness are to be found in unresolved conflicts in Christian theology, and (3) his argument that human self-assertion is a necessary response to the disintegration of Scholasticism and Nominalism.

Löwith and Secularization

At the beginning of *The Legitimacy of the Modern Age,* Blumenberg claims that the controversy over secularization and the related notion of historical progress has had a protracted dogmatizing effect since its first appearance in the late 1940s. The particular focus of Blumenberg's criti-

---

1. The two works best known to English speakers have been translated by Robert M. Wallace: *Work on Myth* (Cambridge, Mass.: MIT Press, 1985), and *The Legitimacy of the Modern Age* (Cambridge, Mass.: MIT Press, 1983). Quotations from *The Legitimacy of the Modern Age* are cited with page numbers in the text. Since its translation into English, this book has been the subject of essays, reviews, and professional meetings of historians, philosophers, religious and literary scholars, and political scientists. For a list of works most directly relevant to the study, see the Bibliography.

cism is on Karl Löwith's work, especially *Meaning in History*.[2] Löwith challenged the claims of Voltaire and other founders of the modern age by arguing that their concept of progress is a secularized form of *Heilsgeschichte,* "salvation history." According to Löwith, the Christian tradition introduced into Western thought the concept of historical progress leading toward the Eschaton—the end of human struggle and the beginning of a perpetual period of happiness and fulfillment. The differences between secular progress and *Heilsgeschichte* are that the fulfillment of history occurs within the here and now (*saeculum*) rather than in the hereafter, and that salvation is accomplished by humankind's actions, not by God's. The term *illegitimacy* is applied to secularization for two reasons. First, history is not a realm over which humankind has total control as the philosophes claimed. It is, therefore, not a realm that humankind can direct toward social and political utopia. Second, it is illegitimate in denying its Christian origins. This denial creates a false concept of the modern age as an epoch founded on reason and set apart from theology and religion. Blumenberg's counterposition challenges the equation Löwith makes between Christianity's concept of a transcendent Kingdom of God and the secularist's dream of world-immanent perfection, arguing that Löwith fails to document the historical process of the transformation in the epochal transition from the medieval to the modern period.

Blumenberg then moves from criticism of Löwith to a more general analysis of secularization as a "category of historical wrong."[3] According to his analysis, the concept of secularization has, from the outset, been based upon a wrongheaded assumption that the essence of Christianity was transformed and perverted during the transition from the medieval to the modern period. Blumenberg challenges this position with a unique, provocative argument that medieval Christianity itself alters the original substance of Christianity and takes the decisive step in secularizing gospel Christianity. Early Christianity, as the gospels clearly demonstrate, was eschatological, since it was awaiting the imminent end of the world. When the eschaton did not occur shortly after the Crucifixion and Resurrection, believers had to organize themselves for survival in

---

2. Karl Löwith, *Meaning in History: The Theological Implications of the Philosophy of History* (Chicago: University of Chicago Press, 1949). A more detailed treatment is offered in *Weltgeschichte und Heilsgeschehen: Die theologischen Voraussetzungen der Geschichtsphilosophie,* 2d ed. (Stuttgart: Kohlhammer, 1953).

3. This phrase is taken from the title of part 1 of *The Legitimacy of the Modern Age* (see 1–124).

8   The Modern Age and the Recovery of Ancient Wisdom

the world. What is more, the need to proselytize the gentile world made it necessary to translate a *kerygma* conceived in the Jewish tradition into the categories of Greek philosophy and religion. These necessities, according to Blumenberg, are the actual source of secularization because they require that the original Christian substance be modified to conform to the Church's mission in the here and now (*saeculum*).

Blumenberg's relocation of the beginnings of secularization in Christendom's effort to accommodate itself to life in the world is more than a clever rhetorical inversion of the usual debate. It sets the context for his provocative reexamination of the conceptual difficulties and the theological dilemmas posed by the effort to integrate Christian eschatology with the prevalent cosmological views of the Hellenistic period. As Blumenberg puts it, "The world, which turned out to be more persistent than expected, attracted once again the old questions regarding its origin and its dependability and demanded a decision between trust and mistrust, an arrangement of life with the world rather than against it" (131). According to Blumenberg, this effort at reconciliation of eschatology with cosmology introduces the fundamental metaphysical questions that have occupied philosophy and theology from the Hellenistic period to the present and are the keys to understanding modern epochal consciousness. Because this is a crucial part of Blumenberg's argument, it must be developed in detail.

Platonic and Gnostic Cosmologies and Christian Theodicy

The two cosmologies that Christianity had to come to terms with were the classical philosophical (Platonic-Aristotelian-Stoic) and the Gnostic. In the Platonic view, "The cosmos is everything that can be, and the Platonic myth of the demiurge guarantees that in the world the potential of everything that could be and of every way in which it could be is exhausted by the reproduction of the Ideas" (127). In this conception, the imperfections and shortcomings of the world derive from two sources: the Platonic demiurge is not omnipotent and does not have the advantage of creating *ex nihilo*. He is confronted instead with a preexistent matter. The point to be noted for later reference is that the problem of evil (*malum*) in the world is not attributable to God in this system. Evil results from the incongruity between matter and Idea, necessity and reason (see 127–32).

Gnosticism, on the other hand, presents a very different explanation of the prevalence of evil in the cosmos. In Gnosticism, the demiurge, who creates the world, is not a benign, limited, lesser deity; he is a malevolent power intent on imprisoning man's spirit in corrupt matter. This conception is obviously at odds with the Platonic view of the cosmos as the full embodiment of all reality; the cosmos is a material order opposed to salvation, the means of accomplishing man's fall—his alienation and the loss of his soul. Moreover, the demiurge has become the principle of evil, the opponent of the transcendent God of salvation. This transcendent God, who loves man and cares for his soul, has nothing to do with creation, except to intervene in an effort to save man from imprisonment in it (see 128-29).

According to Blumenberg, the challenge of Gnosticism is brought directly to Christianity during the time of its dogmatic formation by the heretic Marcion, who was excommunicated in 144 A.D. Marcion's heresy stems from his differentiation of the Old Testament God of the creation from the New Testament God of redemption. The Old Testament God is identified with the evil demiurge who created the world and gave man a law that could not be complied with. The New Testament God is identified as the transcendent Savior who rescues man from a disordered world. Salvation, in this view, depends on man's enlightenment regarding his fundamental and impenetrable deception by the cosmos and his recognition that the transcendent Redeemer is not the same as the creator god. According to Blumenberg, Marcion made this juxtaposition because he "wanted a god who did not need to contradict himself by creating man in such a way that he would have to deliver him from his lost state" (129-30).

Christendom's response to the Gnostic challenge dramatically demonstrates the fundamental problem that secularization (accommodation to the here and now) posed for the Church. The delay of the Parousia forces the Church to "retrieve the world as the creation from the negative role assigned to it by the [Gnostic] doctrine of its demiurgic origin, and to salvage the dignity of the ancient cosmos [of classical philosophy] for its role in the Christian system" (130).

In Blumenberg's view, the early Church's effort to resolve the problem of evil with theological absolutism was short-lived and resulted in "the second coming of Gnosticism" in the form of Nominalism. Nominalism's effort to establish God's absolute transcendence removed Him from the world and from the human condition. Man was left to confront the world on his own and had no choice but to take control of his destiny through modern self-assertion. This line of argument must be developed in some detail.

Augustine and the Problem of Evil

In order for Augustine to defend the goodness of creation against the Gnostic heresy, he had to be able to attribute the prevalence of evil to a source other than the biblical Creator-God. Moreover, since God creates *ex nihilo,* evil or disorder cannot be attributed to inherent flaws in the preexisting material of creation. Given these constraints, Blumenberg argues that Augustine has only one option in formulating his theodicy: "With a gesture just as stirring as it was fateful, he took for man and upon man the responsibility for the burden oppressing the world" (133). This point is crucial to Blumenberg's thesis and must be clearly understood. To justify God, Augustine formulates a new configuration of concepts—freedom, original sin, and providence—which explain how man is responsible for evil and why God is justified in not intervening in the world to rescue mankind. In other words, Blumenberg contends that Augustine resolves the theological challenge of Gnosticism by substituting the sins of man for the wickedness of the Gnostic demiurge.[4]

> In the very text that had convinced Marcion of the wickedness of the Old Testament lawgiver, in Paul's Epistle to the Romans, Augustine found the theological means by which to formulate the dogma of man's universal guilt and to conceive of man's "justification" [in the theological sense of the term] as an absolution that is granted by way of an act of grace and that does not remove from the world the consequences of that guilt. There he also found the doctrine of absolute predestination, which restricted this grace to the small number of the chosen and thus left the continuing guilt of the all too many to explain the lasting corruption of the world. (134–35; brackets in original)

This tactic, according to Blumenberg, attains its immediate objective: Augustine resolves the tensions between the God of creation and the God of salvation. It leaves other questions about man, the world, and God unresolved, however, and they resurface in the conflicts between Scholasticism and Nominalism.

Nominalism and Theological Absolutism

Scholasticism attempted to preserve the ancient cosmos by appropriating Aristotle's proofs of the necessary uniqueness of the cosmos as the

---

4. As we shall see, the substitution of man for the demiurge is a recurrent theme in Blumenberg's analysis and has a key role in his discussion of modern "self-assertion."

full embodiment of space, matter, and forms. At the same time, however, Scholasticism also drew upon Aristotelian concepts to exonerate God from responsibility for humanity's condition in the world. "When High Scholasticism sought to interpret and systematize the biblical God with the categories of the Aristotelian 'thought thinking itself,' the unmoved mover, the *actus purus* [pure act], it had to retract each step of the divine interest in man . . . and make the facts of human history appear as too 'trivial' even to serve as 'occasions' for divine action" (175; translator's brackets). The eventual result of the application of Aristotelian metaphysical principles, so that God's basic concern in each of his acts can only be with himself, was that the basic theological principles of the creation of the world and the redemption of man became secondary.

> The price of this preservation of the cosmos was not only the guilt that man was supposed to assign himself for the condition in which he found the world but also the resignation . . . of any attempt to change for his benefit, through action, a reality for the adversity of which he had himself to blame. The senselessness of self-assertion was the heritage of the Gnosticism which was not overcome but only "translated." (136)

This "second coming" of Gnosticism occurs in the Nominalist response to Scholasticism.

If Scholasticism adopted metaphysical principles that called into question God's role in human affairs, Nominalism called into question the rational dependability of the world. According to Blumenberg, the 1277 A.D. condemnation of the Aristotelian notion that the world was unique as a restriction of God's omnipotence "marks the exact point in time when the interest in the rationality and human intelligibility of creation cedes priority to the speculative fascination exerted by the theological predicates of absolute power and freedom" (160). Of course, Nominalism's purpose in challenging the rationality of the world was to make man uncomfortable with the creation in order to direct him toward salvation outside the world and outside reason. The Nominalist effort to defend God's omnipotence, however, is framed within the rejection of the Aristotelian proof of the rationality of the world. The realist concept of the *universale ante rem* (universal having an existence prior to things) as that which is repeated at will in concrete things makes sense only if the universe represents a finite embodiment of what is possible. The Nominalist concept of the *potentia absoluta* (complete, absolute power), however, implies that there is no limit to what is possible and makes the interpretation of the individual as the repetition of a universal meaningless (see 153). Furthermore, the very richness of creative abundance implies that it can no longer be expected to exhibit any adaptation to the needs of reason (see 154). This, in turn, means that the world no longer possessed an accessible order and was not connected to man's salvation.

The logic of theological absolutism ultimately brings the Scholastic cosmos into question, and the late Middle Ages mark the end of that epochal idea of order. Early modern man, therefore, confronts the same situation as the early Gnostics. He recognizes the error of attachment to the cosmos and its God and knows that he must search for new modes of knowledge. The modern response, however, is different from the Gnostic in one fundamental way. His loss of confidence in the order of the cosmos and his diminished hope of transcendent salvation create a radical alternative: "the immanent self-assertion of reason through the mastery and alteration of reality" (137).

In the ancient and medieval periods, humanity understood itself to be part of a hierarchy of being, the world was rational and knowable, and happiness depended on knowledge of the ordained boundaries of human existence. In the modern age, man's inability to know God or the world, and the failure of reason to obtain truth, forces man into action, i.e., to shape the world to his needs and to create the prospects for happiness and fulfillment. Robert M. Wallace describes this ironic, modern consequence of theological absolutism this way: "So teleology, substantial forms, cosmic order, providence—the dominant concepts of ancient philosophy—are all ruled out. Self-preservation, self-reliance, exploration, experiment, technique, method become the new bywords."[5]

The early modern rebellion of absolute immanence against theological absolutism also rejects the medieval correlation between knowledge and happiness. Nominalism had made a distinction between God's absolute creative potential and the world. This securing of God's absolute transcendence, of course, destroys the classical confidence in the cosmos. The world can no longer be understood as the best and unsurpassable instance of what is possible as material appearance.

> If, then, for nominalism the actual world could not be deduced from the premises of a world in general or from the principle of the best possible world, the radical question arose whether it was necessary or even important for man to know which of the possible world models had been realized in his world, what nature the hidden God has concealed in His creation. But that the hidden truth was a matter of indifference could not in itself signify man's happiness because . . . for the Middle Ages, in all their phases, no concept of happiness was thinkable that could be defined as the mere elimination of negative factors—pain, the affects, insecurity due to

---

5. Robert M. Wallace, "Hans Blumenberg on Descartes and the Modern Age," *Annals of Scholarship* 5 (Fall 1987): 45.

uncertainty. For such a concept of happiness would have made the bliss of the elect in the vision of God into a sort of superfluous addition to a situation, already sufficient unto itself, of freedom from suffering and care. (199)

This condition requires a fundamental adjustment to the correlation between the possession of truth and the attainment of happiness, and this adjustment is apparent in the new stance taken by Descartes. The freedom to abstain from categorical judgment presupposes that man does not require insight into the plan of creation in order to find purpose and happiness in existence. It does, however, require that man "assert himself in existence" in order to create the conditions conducive to his welfare.

. . . the disappearance of the teleological protections that had been part of the concept of nature means that man has to adjust himself to coming to terms with a nature that is not adjusted for his benefit, so as to anticipate the inconsiderateness of natural processes and to make up for the inadequacy of their products by his own production. *Hypothesis*, which from one point of view is the formal expression of the renunciation of the claim to truth in the traditional sense of adequacy [*adaequatio*], becomes from another point of view a means of self-assertion, the potential for human production of that which nature makes scarce or does not provide for man at all. To this kind of theory, which no longer has to provide man's happiness immediately as truth, the *given* reality is more than a matter of indifference only insofar as the theory projects upon it the reality *to be produced* and checks the latter, once produced, against it. Man's existence in the world now has only a mediated relation to theory. (199–200; translator's brackets)

Blumenberg describes the epistemological transformation as the beginning of the end of traditional anthropocentrism and the emergence of a new form of human assertion in which man must function demiurgically.

The Transformation of Human Nature

Traditional anthropocentrism rested upon confidence in the centrality of man in the cosmos and upon confidence in the cosmos as an order created for mankind. For modern man, however, "the world is not reliably arranged in advance for man's benefit, neither is the truth about it any longer at his disposal" (205). In such a world man refines his ability to enjoy nature's benefits by supplying himself with theoretical knowledge that is a precondition of existence in conformity with nature, "but already he does this reserving the right to interfere in nature, to subjugate it as the substrate of demiurgic production" (209). The anthropological consequence, therefore, of theological absolutism and the infinity of God's creative activity is the divinization of man as the demiurge who faces the possibility and the necessity of completing an unfinished world, a world that must still be shaped toward human needs and capacities for enjoyment: "The 'unfinished world' becomes the metaphor of a teleology that discovers reason as its own immanent rule that up until then had been projected onto nature. Only when the mechanism of this projection is exposed does the history of the disappearance of inherited purposes enter the phase of conscious and deliberate destruction" (214). This new awareness of the need to transform knowledge from *adequatio* to *actio* is the key development in modern self-consciousness and modern historical consciousness.[6]

The modern emphasis on self-assertion, then, emerges from the theological and metaphysical problems set in motion by Christianity's efforts to exonerate God from responsibility for the conditions of worldly existence. The effort to defend against Gnosticism leads inevitably to the destruction of the ancient idea of the cosmos and of an intelligible order of reality. The destruction of confidence in an intelligible world oriented to man had to mean an immanently pragmatic change in man's understanding of and relation to the world. This is primarily a change from a passive knowledge of the given order of reality to an active creation of reality. The transformation leads, in turn, to a new concept of human freedom (see 137–39). Augustine had imposed freedom on man as a way of exonerating God for the condition of the world. By imposing freedom on man Augustine makes man responsible for the evil present in the world. But the burden of freedom imposed by the theological absolutism of Nominalism has a quite different consequence. According to Blumenberg, "It is responsibility for the condition of the world as a challenge relating to the future, not as an original offense in the past" (137).

This new historical consciousness of an open future also transforms the understanding of evil. The bad aspects of the world no longer appear

---

6. Blumenberg attempts to demonstrate that modern man's "divinization" is not the result of secularization; that is, modern self-assertion is not a defiant effort at self-divinization, but the complementary component of theological absolutism. This analysis offers an alternative origin of progress, since progress is not secularized *heilsgeschichte*—it is the outcome of theological absolutism and the "unfinished world" confronting man. Blumenberg's analysis encounters difficulties, however, because his notions of human creativity and of science and technology are not compatible with the mechanistic world model, which is not susceptible to human manipulation (see *The Legitimacy of the Modern Age*, 217). Manipulating the mechanical order is important in the discussion of the *prisca theologia* and the development of science in chapters 6 and 7.

as metaphysical marks of the quality of the world principle or of punishing justice, but as a contingent state of affairs. Because these deficiencies and shortcomings are contingent and can be altered in conformity with human need and creative adaptation, the parameters of the basic impulse toward self-preservation are also transformed. Self-preservation is pulled "out of its biologically determined normality, where it went unnoticed and turned into the 'theme' of human self-comprehension" (139). Integral to this self-comprehension and self-assertion is the growth and acceleration of technicity: "In the growth of the technical sphere there lives, consciously facing an alienated reality, a will to extort from this reality a new 'humanity.'" This new effort to shape the world to human needs, as already noted, is the ironic result of the effort to overcome Gnosticism. "Gnosticism had made acute the problem of the quality of the world for man and, through the contradiction that the patristic literature and the Middle Ages opposed to it, made *cosmodicy* conditional on *theodicy*. The modern age attempted to strike out this condition by basing its *anthropodicy* on the world's lack of consideration of man, on its inhuman order" (142).

The self-assertion of modern man therefore depends upon a fundamental shift in the concept of knowledge (*actio* vs. *adequatio*) and its relation to happiness. According to Blumenberg, modern man had to "reconstruct the connection between cognitive truth and finding happiness in a different way if, following Francis Bacon's new formula, domination over nature was to be a precondition of the recovery of paradise" (232). This reorientation was prompted by the medieval destruction of the theoretical pretension to truth and the conviction that only truth could provide a guarantee of happiness. Blumenberg offers a vivid characterization of the modern outcome.

> The necessity [*Notwendigkeit*] of self-preservation becomes the versatility [*Wendigkeit*] of self-assertion, and what was a mere occupation becomes a prerogative to be secured and at the same time becomes the energy that increases exponentially each time it turns out that the suspected reservation of the unknown but knowable does exist—that knowledge can extend beyond the Pillars of Hercules, beyond the limits of normal optics and the postulate of visibility, in other words, beyond the horizons that had been assigned to man as long as he had thought that he could remain the onlooker in repose, the leisurely enjoyer of the world, taken care of by providence. (234; translator's brackets)

The transformation of man into an active shaper of the world required a fundamental change in attitude toward the world. For Blumenberg this change is best revealed by examining the transformation of the attitude toward curiosity (*curiositas*) about the world from ancient philosophy and theology to its theoretical rehabilitation in the modern age. The theoretical issues that emerge in Blumenberg's treatment of this theme are central to the rest of this study and must be considered in detail. To explain this shift, Blumenberg must again rework the historical lines from the ancient to the modern period.

Curiosity in Ancient Thought

The break separating the ancient world of myth from the beginnings of classical philosophy occurred when the Pre-Socratics made observation of the heavens the exemplary exercise of man's vocation for theory—that is, when they recognized in the beauty of heaven's objects indirect evidence of divinity. Aristotle gave this development its well-known formulation in the Metaphysics: "All men by nature strive to know." Implicit in this Aristotelian claim are two related notions: (1) there is a cognitive relationship between the inquiring soul and the divine ordering principles behind the world and (2) contemplation of eternal truth is the source of self-realization and happiness. This is, however, only one of the developments that characterize classical philosophy. The other is found in the Socratic shift from contemplation of the heavens to the daily duties of the citizen of the polis. This turning toward self-knowledge and the immediate problems of justice and virtue sets up a fundamental tension in philosophy as to whether the Pre-Socratic natural philosophy must be disqualified as a distraction from the primary aim of philosophy or whether it "must be coordinated with that primacy of the knowledge of the human, as the precondition of man's integrating himself into the cosmos" (246).

Blumenberg traces the tensions surrounding the "Socratic turning" as it develops in Xenophon, the Cynics, and Cicero, on the one hand, and Plato on the other (see 247–59). In Xenophon's interpretation, all knowledge is justified by its utility and the objects of theoretical inquiry are similarly gauged by their contribution to action. Plato, however, in the *Phaedo* and the *Timaeus*, integrates self-knowledge and theoretical knowledge. The Platonic portrait of Socrates also emphasizes his interest in the cosmos as a way to juxtapose Socratic philosophy to Sophism.

> The Socratic formula of the identity of wisdom and morality, of knowledge and virtue, can be understood as the overcoming of Sophism by its own means. The freeing of knowledge from its pragmatic employment in the service of political interests, the recovery of its immanent significance, gives to action a norm that is independent of partial ends. But this means

that the objectivity of theory cannot be regulated primarily through the selection of an interest, which seeks only to procure justifications and techniques for its success. On the contrary, it must seek to grasp the universal order whose maintenance alone guarantees to human action that it draws after it eudemonia as the confirmation of its correctness. The appropriateness that governs action as its norm can no longer be defined as the pragmatic coordination of the means to particular occasional ends but rather as the subordination of all ends and means to the single highest end of man, that of achieving and maintaining his well-being within the cosmos. (252–53)

This Socratic view, therefore, links knowledge of nature (the ordained conditions of existence) to man's self-knowledge (knowledge of the ordained nature of man and the prescribed sources of human happiness and fulfillment).

Two Platonic concepts further embellish this Socratic view, the doctrine of Ideas and the linking of human knowledge to demiurgic activity. "The Platonic doctrine of the Ideas very rapidly lost its original limitation to concepts having force in logic and ethics and broadened the sphere of Ideas into the world of the original images of everything in existence" (253–54). In the process of the broadening, the cosmos is divested of its foreignness and sheer externality. As a result, it is no longer possible to draw a distinction between man's essential concerns and what in the guise of nature appears only to stimulate his curiosity: "The doctrine of Ideas not only *explains* man's learning and inquiry as turning to the truth possession already latent within him; it also *legitimates* them as the exhaustion of a potential that would otherwise remain untouched" (254). Plato also provides an explicit legitimation of man's claim to knowledge with the myth of the demiurge. "He has the world fabricator produce the human soul from the material left over from the making of the world soul and thus, through its kinship with the substance of the world soul, guarantee it universal access to knowledge"—down to having the number of human souls correspond to the number of stars (254).

Aristotle draws upon Platonic concepts and myth but gives a different emphasis to human striving for knowledge. According to Blumenberg, the *Metaphysics* asserts that man's "essential nature justifies itself simply by being realized and has no need of relation to any other existential purpose. The naturalness of the cognitive drive is read directly from man's relation to the perceptual world, from the delight he takes in his access to it through the senses" (255). Aristotle separates this theoretical knowledge from practical concerns about life in the world. Theoretical speculation does not arise in conjunction with pragmatic problems of existence, but after the necessities of life have been met. Therefore, pure knowledge in this view is a goal in and of itself that is related to human freedom and to human self-realization. In another passage Aristotle rejects the poets' claims that the gods are jealous of man and argues that the life of pure theory and of perfect happiness is only possible for man because of the divine reason that inhabits man. This Aristotelian claim is transmitted into Scholastic thought through Averroës, who claimed Aristotle was created and given to men by divine providence in order to reveal what man can know (see 255–57).

The philosophical attitude toward theoretical curiosity undergoes further development and reformulation in the Hellenistic period. Stoicism continues the basic views of Aristotle, while Epicureanism and Skepticism contend that theoretical curiosity is a source of fear or false hope that frustrates human happiness and disorients the search for self-knowledge. Gnosticism also challenges the idea of an ordered cosmos and juxtaposes curiosity about nature to knowledge that leads to salvation. Within this context patristic theology developed its position. The key figure, especially for subsequent developments, is Augustine, who is critical of excessive philosophical curiosity. Interest in and attraction to nature can derail the search for enduring happiness in God, and it can lead to infatuation with one's own theoretical skills. As a prevention against curiosity, God intervenes supernaturally into the lawful workings of nature to remind man that his knowledge can never be exact and that nature is not wholly knowable or predictable. To Augustine, the exact measurement and mathematical prediction of astronomical data tends to seduce man into impious pride by making him forget that this extraordinary accomplishment is dependent on the cosmic order and man's God-given rationality (349).

Scholasticism and the Rehabilitation of Theoretical Curiosity

Scholasticism considered no measure applicable to the world other than God's own and therefore did not believe man capable of knowing the measure of the world or of making use of it. The seeking of too much knowledge (being too curious) is, of course, identified as the cause of man's downfall in the biblical myth of Eden, and it remained a key issue in the Middle Ages. Thomas Aquinas identifies original sin as the failure to distinguish curiosity from appropriate interest in the world (*studiositas*), which is necessary because exile from Eden imposed on man the need for appropriate care and purposeful action in the world (331). Thomas also associates curiosity with becoming charmed by the created order and thereby neglectful of the divine origin. Curiosity, especially about nature, must be limited or become a distraction.

The modern rehabilitation of theoretical curiosity required freeing it from this Scholastic characterization as caring for superfluous matters. This rehabilitation begins in Nominalist theology, specifically with the (1) alienation of the certainty of salvation from self-realization and (2) the loss of the world's metaphysical status as an expression of divine providence or natural revelation.[7] "Raising theology to its maximal pretension over against reason had the unintended result of reducing theology's role in explaining the world to a minimum," thereby transforming the role of reason and destroying the foundation of Scholastic rational cosmology and theology. Consequently, what was intended as a defense of theology contributes a new status to man's care for the world and curiosity is transformed from a superfluous distraction into a necessity.

> The element of *cura* [care] in *curiositas* now becomes the very root of its meaning, which legitimizes the cognitive appetite as the attentiveness that is provoked by the world. The modern age began, not indeed as the epoch of the death of God, but as the epoch of the hidden God, the *deus absconditus*—and a hidden God is *pragmatically* as good as dead. The nominalist theology induces a human relation to the world whose implicit content could have been formulated in the postulate that man had to behave as though God were dead. This induces a restless taking stock of the world, which can be designated as the motive power of the age of science. (346; translator's brackets)

According to this analysis, science emerges when theory abandons the assumption that the creation must be known and understood from the angle of vision and with the categories of the Creator. The next step occurs with Galileo's scientific inventions, which further destroy the idea of a finite, rationally ordered cosmos.

> Galileo's use of the telescope marks a historical moment whose unsuspected result, the discovery of unseen realities in the universe, was to have radical consequences for the understanding of man's position in and toward nature. The most important consequence was that (so to speak) 'curiosity is rewarded'—the weighty significance of what had hitherto been withheld from man is confirmed, and thus the morality of self-restriction is disabused and put in the wrong, and its abandonment is a logical consequence. (369)

---

7. These developments also undercut the classic argument for an ordained connection between the knowable world and man's sensory organs, especially sight. This is therefore a further destruction of the anthropocentric cosmos.

These developments so fundamentally alter the basic assumption about man's condition in the world that they require a mythic reconfiguration, which Bacon supplies in *Valerius terminus*. The key passage offers a reinterpretation of original sin. According to Bacon, God had given man dominion of the world at creation; therefore, God intended man to have the knowledge and the power to live a paradisiacal existence. This state was destroyed, however, by man's inappropriate desire for the deepest divine secrets of morality and therefore of salvation and damnation. As a result of the fall, man plunges into a state of intellectual lassitude in which he confuses the prohibition against knowledge of salvation with the permissible knowledge of nature and erroneously creates the classical, metaphysical concepts of knowledge that emphasize man's passive contemplation. Bacon's own age, however, marks the beginning of a proper reorientation to God and a proper reorientation to the world, and the orientation leads to an active role in dominating nature and improving the human condition. This new orientation underscores the appropriateness of curiosity. In fact, Bacon inverts the traditional prohibition and makes lack of curiosity a moral flaw and ultimately a rejection of man's God-given responsibility. This same theme is present in the *Novum Organum*, and Bacon adds to this remythologizing by pointing to the crossing of ancient boundaries in the frontispiece of the *Instauratio magna*, which shows a ship sailing past the Pillars of Hercules, the limits of the known, habitable world.[8]

The self-consciousness of the modern age found in the image of the Pillars of Hercules and their order, *Nec plus ultra* [No further], which Dante's Odysseus still understood (and disregarded) as meaning "Man may not venture further here," the symbol of its new beginning and of its claim directed against what had been valid until then. On the title page of Bacon's *Instauratio magna* [*Great Renewal*] of 1620, Odysseus's ship was to appear behind the Pillars of Hercules, interpreted by this self-confident motto: *Multi pertransibunt et augibetur scientia* [Many will pass through and knowledge will be increased]. And in 1668 one of the first attempts to draw up a balance sheet of the new age of science will appear under the title *Plus ultra* [Further yet]. (340; translator's brackets)

We have now reached a point at which we can draw together the fundamental elements of Blumenberg's analysis and begin to relate it to issues raised by the *prisca theologia* tradition.

---

8. Blumenberg develops the next stage of the transcendence of boundaries in a chapter on Feuerbach and Freud, who direct the voyage inward and challenge the metaphysical notions of reason and of order. An analysis of key Baconian images and symbols is provided in chapter 7 below.

Summary

Blumenberg's legitimization of modernity depends on a defense of three of its fundamental aspects: self-assertion, the concept of progress, and the linking of theoretical knowledge of nature with the technological power to control and to improve the human condition. Blumenberg's historical and theoretical analysis attempts to demonstrate that self-assertion is not an arrogant defiance of Christian theology. Instead, it is the logical and necessary outgrowth of the theological absolutism of the late Middle Ages. Similarly, progress is not a concept that is created by the transformation of Christian *Heilsgeschichte* into a world-immanent doctrine of salvation. The concept emerges, instead, from two fundamental developments. The first occurs through technological developments in the early modern period that literally open the horizons and perspectives that had seemed to be impenetrable. The telescope, for example, breaks the boundaries of the finite cosmos and destroys the fundamental distinction between the sublunar and the heavenly realms. Technological advances also permit the navigation that opens the world and breaks down the boundary between the inhabited world and the boundless and unknown (*okeanos*). In light of these developments, it is no longer a dangerous and defiant act to sail past the boundaries of the Pillars of Hercules.

These events have a fundamental impact on the Western understanding of cosmology, anthropology, epistemology, and history. Metaphysical speculation, particularly under the weight of Nominalism's theological absolutism, had broken the interconnection between the knowable cosmos, man's reason, and God's nature and purpose. It replaced the familiar interrelationships with concepts of an infinite and ultimately unknowable cosmos, an absolute, omniscient God whose acts are ultimately unknowable to mankind, and a human nature that is disenfranchised from any direct knowledge of or influence on God's grace. When the traditional philosophical and theological epistemology disintegrates, the modern emphasis on theoretical knowledge as a human ordering activity and on instrumental knowledge as the means for human mastery of the world become both possible and necessary. Theoretical knowledge, however, becomes utilitarian rather than absolute.

This epistemological shift is the result of another fundamental transformation between the modern age and previous ages, the transformation of curiosity—caring for the world. In a world that is indifferent to man, man must care for the situation he finds himself in and must care for himself and find an appropriate means of contending with the conditions of existence. This new emphasis on care and on curiosity in turn contributes further to the importance of self-assertion and opens up further dimensions of the prospects of progress.

Blumenberg's Work in Light of Recent Research

To this point, discussion of Blumenberg has been more descriptive than analytical; now, however, an evaluation of Blumenberg's reinterpretation can be begun. This examination will not focus on the infrastructure of his argument; instead, it will concentrate on the question of the adequacy and the thoroughness of Blumenberg's acquaintance with and utilization of research that has a direct bearing on his reinterpretation. More specifically, the evaluation will center on the thoroughness of Blumenberg's acquaintance with fundamental research into basic elements of his historical reconstruction, that is, the generative ideas and the major thinkers contributing to the epochal shifts that produce the modern emphasis on self-assertion, progress, and knowledge as power. Of course, the posing of the question in itself implies that there are significant omissions, and my Introduction has already indicated that the most important area of omission is research on the influence of the *prisca theologia* tradition upon the main lines of Renaissance thought. Therefore, it is appropriate to examine Blumenberg's treatment—or lack of treatment—of these developments.

At the time Blumenberg was formulating his theories, there was a significant new emphasis in Renaissance scholarship that was widely known and did have a significant bearing on the fundamental motifs that Blumenberg was interested in analyzing. In his book, *Spiritual and Demonic Magic* (1958), D. P. Walker referred to this aspect of the Renaissance as the revival of the *prisca theologia,* or Ancient Wisdom tradition. The emphasis on the Ancient Wisdom is tied directly to a resurgence of interest in Plato and Neoplatonism and to the accessibility of materials from Byzantium as well as the works of its scholars. This Platonic or Neoplatonic tradition is an exceptionally elastic framework that includes a variety of pseudoscientific and esoteric religious traditions that were accumulated, incorporated, and refined between the establishment of the Neoplatonic School in Alexandria in late antiquity and its transmission into Italy during the Renaissance. While this is a wide-ranging esoteric tradition, it is clear that Ficino, the founder of the Platonic Academy sponsored by the Medici family, was drawn to those elements that seemed to offer a "new understanding of human nature."[9] As the term *prisca*

---

9. In the dedicatory preface to his *Theologia Platonica* (*Opera Omnia*, 4 vols., 2d.

theologia indicates, Ficino and other scholars of the time regarded this tradition as containing primary revelations that God gave to the most ancient and wisest men of the Near East and Mediterranean.[10] In the next chapter the content of these materials will be discussed in detail; here, however, it is necessary only to note that they have an important bearing on two of Blumenberg's key themes.

First, Blumenberg focuses on the points of transition in the major epochal shifts from the classical to the medieval and from the medieval to the modern worlds. In the first transition, Blumenberg gives detailed attention to the philosophical and theological developments occurring in the Hellenistic period as significant transition points from the original formulations of Plato and Aristotle to their adoption, adaptation, and transmission in subsequent generations. These developments are important in their own right but are particularly important in relation to Blumenberg's analysis because they set the context within which Christianity must accommodate its fundamental cosmology, theology, and anthropology. Blumenberg gives special attention to the challenge of Gnosticism. As programs of saving knowledge, these elements of Ancient Wisdom are also gnostic in the broad, general sense of the term: their myths and root symbols attempt to account for the disorder and alienation in the present age and promise deliverance through saving knowledge. Although some of this tradition expresses the same radical, dualistic beliefs found in early Christianity and Gnosticism, there are also immanentist constructions that present an entirely different conception. In these myths, the present state of disorder can be overcome through mankind's rediscovery of its role as a terrestrial god.

In one of the key texts repeatedly referred to in the Renaissance, God creates man and empowers him with the knowledge of the workings of nature so that he can participate directly in the creation of the natural world and can use his knowledge of nature's power to create a paradise on earth.[11] This material is extremely important for Blumenberg's analysis of the evolution of early modern cosmology and anthropology be-

---

ed. [Basel, 1576; reprint, Turin: Bottega d'Erasmo, 1959], 2:562), Ficino indicates that he is setting out a new understanding of human nature, which, as the title suggests, is drawn from Platonic thought. As already noted, "Platonic" is an elastic term that includes a number of occult traditions, especially the Hermetic materials.

10. This marks a significant difference from the Latin humanist tradition. The humanist recovery of ancient learning is associated with the *studia humanitatis*. The Greek *prisca theologia* tradition is associated with the recovery of ultimate, metaphysical truth.

11. This myth is in the *Corpus Hermeticum;* it is analyzed in detail in the next chapter.

cause its saving knowledge is aimed at transforming the disorder in nature through human action. This knowledge does not provide an escape from the prison of the world, but empowers man to transform the conditions of existence through action in history. What is particularly important about these materials is that they offer a reconciliation of the problem to which Blumenberg gives so much attention: the dilemma of the creator God versus the redeemer God. In these myths God creates a perfect macrocosm and endows man with the power to create an equally perfect microcosm. The myths never fully account for the disorder that disrupts the harmonious relation, but it is never attributed to God. Moreover, this disorder is temporary and correctable through recovery of the knowledge that a loving God has provided. The Ancient Wisdom also has a particular bearing on Blumenberg's emphasis on curiosity, or care for the world. In this conception, God gives man the knowledge and the authority to care for the world—to completely understand it and to manipulate it for his own purposes. Here again is a concept fundamental to Blumenberg's analysis that lies outside his line of interpretation.

The second reason that the Ancient Wisdom is important for Blumenberg's analysis is that it also reappears at the second threshold, between the medieval and the modern periods. Ficino, whose influence on the early modern period is undeniable, drew heavily on this tradition. As chapter 3 will demonstrate, Ficino reintroduces the Hermetic conception of man as a terrestrial god and restores magic as the God-given knowledge that permits man to operate on the natural world and improve the human condition. This analysis will also show that Ficino's restoration of Hermetic magic is based on a cosmology that is closely connected to developments in science in the sixteenth, seventeenth, and eighteenth centuries. The revival of the *prisca theologia,* therefore, is directly involved in the modern transition phase and influences the work of seminal modern figures. Of course, it would not be appropriate to point to these materials if the new interpretive research had appeared after Blumenberg had formulated his views. This is not the case, however. Walker's work was available, as was that of Frances Yates and Eugenio Garin.[12]

The presence of *prisca theologia* materials and their influence in the early modern period not only have a significant bearing on individual elements of Blumenberg's work but also on his general thesis. His fundamental claim is that the modern period is legitimate because self-assertion, progress, and the accompanying epistemology are legitimate an-

---

12. See the Bibliography for other influential studies published before 1966, when *Die Legitimität der Neuzeit* appeared.

thropological and epistemological counterresponses to the excesses of Nominalism. Drawing on a knowledge of the Ancient Wisdom tradition, however, it is possible to trace an alternate line of development for the same fundamental features. In this complementary pattern, mankind does not assert control of his own destiny in response to the absence of God. In the myths and symbols of the *prisca theologia,* God gives man the role of terrestrial god. Man also does not arrive at his linking of theoretical knowledge with power through the breakdown of the order of the cosmos. Instead, the knowledge to operate on and control nature is given by God. Again, these myths and symbols would not be relevant to Blumenberg's enterprise if their influence were not apparent in major figures in the epochal transitions that Blumenberg analyzes or if they did not supply complementary images, metaphors, and myths for the epochal pattern of modernity that Blumenberg explores.

These materials also challenge other aspects of Blumenberg's approach that need to be briefly identified here and will be developed in greater detail in later stages of the analysis. First, these materials challenge a conventional assumption in Blumenberg's work and that of many interpreters of modernity by calling for the elimination of an either/or approach to the origins of modernity, in which either the Renaissance or the Scientific Revolution is designated as the source of the epochal break from the Middle Ages. The histories that trace the beginnings of modernity to the Renaissance follow the general pattern established by Jacob Burckhardt, who sees in the Renaissance recovery of the classical tradition the reassertion of human dignity and creativity that constitutes the essential character of modern man and creates the distinctive features of modern Western culture. Those who focus on the Scientific Revolution discredit the Renaissance claims as part of a well-intended but ultimately unsuccessful effort to emphasize human self-determination. In this view the beginning of the modern period is found in the developments leading to the Scientific Revolution and the application of the principles of the mathematizing sciences to the social sciences. This approach is, of course, as old as the famous quarrel of the Ancients and Moderns, which gave the fundamental break its categorical differentiation. Advocates of the Ancients were those who clung to the old cosmos, the old epistemology, and the old anthropology much as Blumenberg portrays them. Those favoring the Moderns saw within the principles of science the means of controlling nature and solving social problems. The influence of the *prisca theologia* on both the Renaissance and the Scientific Revolution makes this either/or approach outmoded. The origins of science can now be seen as closely connected to the cosmological and epistemological issues posed in the Neoplatonic/Hermetic Revival.[13]

Another assumption challenged by the *prisca theologia* involves boundaries on the influence of Christian ideas and motifs. Blumenberg still conceives of the Christian influence as reaching its last stages in the formulation of Nominalism and sees subsequent developments as having an origin other than Christianity. Tracing the Hermetic influence makes it clear that many major figures who shaped the modern period were struggling with the influence and significance of the Ancient Wisdom in relation to Christianity well after the Nominalist controversies had subsided. Ficino was a priest who undertook the integration of the Ancient Wisdom in order to show its compatibility with Christianity and to demonstrate the superiority of Christianity. Agrippa, one of the major figures of the sixteenth century, saw in the Ancient Wisdom the means of purifying the disorder within the Church, and Bacon and Newton both believed that the new science was capable of producing a means of fulfilling millennial expectations of traditional Christianity. The interrelationship of religious millenarianism, political utopianism, and the adoption of science to meet social and political objectives in the early modern period points to other significant developments missing in Blumenberg's analysis.

Having identified key points of intersection and diversion between Blumenberg's work and the approach taken here, we can now turn to an analysis of the *prisca theologia* texts and their influence on early modern thought.

---

13. See, for example, works by Allen G. Debus and B. J. T. Dobbs listed in the Bibliography.

2. The Renaissance Revival of the Prisca Theologia

In the preface to his translation of Plotinus, Ficino explains that Cosimo de' Medici conceived of the project of revivifying Platonic thought after hearing the Byzantine scholar Gemistus Pletho's enthusiastic praise of Plato during the Council of Florence (1438-1439).[1] In subsequent years, Cosimo commissioned agents to acquire Platonic and other ancient writings, and in 1462 he gave Ficino a villa at Careggi that was to serve as the site of the new Platonic Academy. Ficino began work on the Platonic texts, intending to provide a complete Latin edition, but in 1463, at the urging of Cosimo, he set aside his work on Plato to prepare a Latin translation of the first fourteen books of the *Corpus Hermeticum,* which Ficino called the *Pimander.*[2]

The reasons for giving primacy to Hermes Trismegistus are made clear in the *argumentum* to the *Pimander.* The *argumentum* begins by establishing Hermes as one of the earliest and greatest of the *prisci theologi.* "Moses was born during the age of Atlas the astrologer, who was the brother of Prometheus the natural philosopher [*physici*] and maternal uncle of Hermes the greater [*majoris*] whose nephew was Hermes Trismegistus. . . . They say that he [Hermes Trismegistus] killed Argus, ruled the Egyptians and gave them laws and letters."[3] In subsequent passages, Ficino notes that Hermes received the title Trismegistus, "Thrice-Great," because he was the greatest philosopher, the greatest priest, and the greatest king ever to have lived, and that he attained such a godlike status that temples were dedicated to him and the open speaking of his name was forbidden.

---

1. Pletho was one of the Byzantine representatives at this council, which was called to consider the reunification of Eastern and Western Christendom. Although the motives for reunification were primarily political, Cosimo was drawn to the theological and philosophical traditions and to the rich collections of ancient documents. He was particularly attracted to the Hermetic materials as a common source for Moses, Pythagoras, and Plato.
2. The *Asclepius,* the second part of the Hermetic writings, was already available in a Latin translation erroneously attributed to Apuleius.
3. I have translated and paraphrased the *argumentum* from *Opera Omnia,* 4 vols., 2d. ed. (Basel, 1576; reprint, Turin: Bottega d'Erasmo, 1959), 4:1836.

Ficino then indicates that Hermes progressed from natural philosophy to study of the gods and finally to contemplation of and teaching about the majesty of God, the orders of demons, and the transmigration (*mutatianibus*) of souls. For that reason, he is called the first author of theology (*Primus igitur theologia appellatus*). Ficino next provides a theological genealogy showing that Hermes is the originator of the Platonic wisdom.

> Orpheus, following Hermes, became the second of the ancient theologians. Aglophemus was initiated into the teachings of Orpheus and was succeeded by Pythagoras in theology, Philolaus, the teacher of our divine Plato, was his disciple. In this way, a *prisca theologia*, completely coherent with itself, was developed by six marvelous theologians, beginning with Hermes and culminating in Plato.[4]

The most important points to note about this genealogy are that it establishes the harmony of the ancient revelations by tracing them to a single line of transmission, and it also traces Plato's teachings to a divine source. Ficino then notes that two of Hermes' writings are most divine, the *Asclepius* and the *Pimander,* and he explains that the purpose of these books is to teach other men how to rise above the deceptions of sense and fantasy and to open their minds to the divine Mind (*Mens*) so that we can contemplate the order of all things as they exist in God.

The next chapter will show how Ficino uses these materials in his *Theologia Platonica* to introduce a "new concept of human nature" that has important implications for the modern self-understanding. Here, however, the focus will be on the key elements of the *prisca theologia* tradition that Ficino spoke of so rapturously. Because of Hermes Trismegistus's exalted position in the genealogy of the *prisca theologia,* we will focus on the teachings in the *Pimander* and *Asclepius* and then compare them with Gnostic and Christian themes in order to relate them to Blumenberg's analysis of the epochal shifts that create modernity.

Hermes becomes the wisest of the Egyptian magi through the revelations made by the divine messenger, Pimander. The first of these revelations in the *Corpus Hermeticum* (Ficino's *Pimander*) is a compact but comprehensive myth of creation. This revelation occurs after a spiritually restless Hermes has struggled to advance beyond normal sensory

---

4. For a useful examination of this and other genealogies of wisdom developed by Ficino, see D. P. Walker, "The Prisca Theologia in France," *Journal of the Warburg and Courtauld Institutes* 17 (1954): 204–59. In every instance Hermes is either first, or he is second to Zoroaster (for example, see the *Theologia Platonica*), or is contemporaneous with him (*Plotinus Commentaries*).

knowledge in order to gain a fuller and more complete understanding of reality. His efforts are rewarded by being called into the presence of Pimander, "the mind of absolute authority," who asks Hermes, "What do you wish to hear and see and, having understood, to learn and know?" Hermes replies, "I want to learn about the things that are, to perceive their nature, and to know God." In response, Pimander changes his form:

> . . . immediately all things opened up to me at once, and I saw a limitless sight. . . . That light, he said, is I, Mind (i.e., Nous), your God, who antedates the moist Nature which appeared out of the darkness. The bright Word from Mind is the son of God. What then, I said? Know this: that which in you sees and hears (i.e., your word) is the Word of the Lord, and the mind (in you) is God the Father (i.e., Father Mind). For they are not separated from each other. Rather, their union is (i.e., constitutes) life. Thank you, I said.[5]

Following this explanation, Pimander directs Hermes to meditate on the light so that he might come to know it.

> With these words he gazed at me for a long time, such that I trembled at the sight of him. Then, when he had raised his head, I beheld in my mind the light which (now) consisted of countless powers and which had (now) become a limitless cosmos. The fire was encompassed by a great power and, having been subdued, stood still. This is what I saw, understanding it through the word(s) of Poimandres. (17)

In other words, Hermes had seen the Mind (*Nous/Mens*), the archetypal form that existed prior to the beginning of the cosmos. Hermes next asks to know the origin of the elements of nature. Pimander tells him that God created the Demiurge, who created the seven celestial Governors who encompass the world and whose rule is known as Fate. The nature of the creation of the world is significant:

> At once the Word of God [Logos] leaped out of the downward hanging elements into the pure (part of the) created (i.e., material) world and was united with the Demiurgical Mind, for it (i.e., Word) was consubstantial

---

5. Robert Segal, *The Poimandres as Myth: Scholarly Theory and Gnostic Meaning*, vol. 33 of *Religion and Reason* (Berlin: Mouton de Gruyter, 1986), 16–17. Subsequent quotations are cited with page numbers in the text. The standard edition of the Hermetic texts is *Corpus Hermeticum*, 4 vols., trans. A. D. Nock and A. J. Festugière (Paris: Société d'édition "Les Belles Lettres," 1954–1960); the text under consideration appears in vol. 4. Ficino's Latin translation and commentary are found in vol. 4 of *Opera Omnia*. See my Bibliography for principal commentaries and interpretations.

(with the Demiurge). The downward hanging elements of Nature were left behind, deprived of reason, so that they were (i.e., became) sheer matter.

Together with the Word, the Demiurgical Mind, encompassing the spheres and spinning them in a whirl, set his creations revolving and let them turn from an indeterminate beginning to an infinite end, for it (i.e., their revolution) begins where it ends. Their revolution, as the Mind wanted, brought forth from the downward hanging elements irrational living beings, for he did not grant them reason: the air brought forth birds, the water fish, and—the earth and the water having been separated from each other, as the Mind wanted—the earth brought forth from herself the animals which it had in itself: quadrupeds and reptiles, both wild and tame beasts. (17-18)

Of particular note is the explanation of the presence in the world of some entities that remain matter and those that are spiritualized by their union with the *Logos* and the *Nous* of the Demiurge. This description will be important to compare to Blumenberg's description of the tension between the myth of the cosmos and the Gnostic myth of creation; but for now, it is important to develop other components of the myth.

Having had the nature of the creation revealed to him, Hermes is next told of man's creation. The first important feature is that the Supreme God—not the Noetic Demiurge—is man's creator. "But the Mind, the Father of all, who is life and light, brought forth a (Primal) Man (i.e., Anthropos) equal to himself. He loved Man as his own son, for he (i.e., Man) was very beautiful, since he possessed the image of his Father. Actually, it was his own form which God loved. He (i.e., God) handed over to him all his creations" (18). When man sees the creation of the Demiurge, he wants to participate in creation and God the Father readily consents.

> So entering the Demiurgical realm, where he was to have full power, he beheld his brother's creations. The Governors loved him, and each gave him a share of his own position. After he had mastered their essence and had received a share of their nature, he wished to break through the bounds of their spheres and to learn well (or: subdue) the power of him who rules over the fire. (18)

After receiving knowledge and creative power from the cosmic sources, man enters into the world of nature and matter.

> So he (i.e., Man) who had full power over the world of mortal beings and irrational living beings bent downward through the harmony (of the spheres), having (already) broken through its exterior, and showed to downward hanging Nature the beautiful form of God. When she saw that

he possessed insatiable beauty and every power of the Governors plus the form of God, she smiled with love. For she saw the image of the most beautiful form of Man in the water and its shadow over the land. When he (in turn) saw the form similar to himself existing in her in the water, he loved it and wished to inhabit it. Immediately with the wish came the deed, and he (thus) inhabited the irrational form. When Nature had received her beloved, she embraced him completely, and they mingled, for they were lovers. (18)

The narrator then explains the implications of this union for man's nature. "For this reason man, distinct from all (other) living beings on earth, is twofold: mortal through the body, immortal through the essential man. For although he is immortal and has power over all, he suffers mortality, for he is subject to Fate" (18-19).

Pimander then reveals a secret of creation that had been hidden. The world existed in this primordial state for an unspecified period, but then God willed it to end and moved the creation to its final stage:

All living beings, being androgynous, were separated at the same time as man. Some became males, others females. Immediately, God, through a sacred word, said: Increase in increase and increase in increase all you creatures and creations. Let him who is thoughtful recognize that he is immortal and that the cause of death is love. And (let him recognize) all things that exist. . . .

When he (i.e., Poimandres) had said this, Providence, through Fate and the harmony (of the spheres), made the intercourses and established the generations, and all things were multiplied according to their species. He who has recognized himself comes into abounding good, but he who, out of the error of love, has loved the body remains in the dark straying, suffering through the senses the things of death. (19-20)

At this point a key question is posed by Hermes: "What sin so great . . . have the ignorant committed to be deprived of immortality?" In an interesting deviation from the question-and-answer mode used thus far, Pimander does not give a direct answer, but tells Hermes that if he has been attentive, he should know the answer. Hermes replies that it is because "prior to the individual body is the gloomy darkness, from which (came) the moist Nature, of which the body was composed in the material world" (20). Pimander asks if he understands how death (loss of immortality) is to be avoided. When Hermes replies that man must turn toward the light (knowledge/*Nous*) because it is the essence of God and the essence of man, Pimander says: "You have spoken well. Light and life are God and Father, from whom Man was born. If, then, you learn that he (i.e., Man) is (composed) of light and life and that you (i.e., narrator) are (composed) of them, you will go back to life" (20). But Hermes is still somewhat troubled, wondering whether all men possess God-given minds and are capable of salvation. Pimander answers that "I myself, Mind, am present with holy, good, pure, merciful, and pious men, and my presence proves helpful to them. . . . But to the foolish, evil, wicked, envious, selfish, murderous, and impious ones I am far away, giving way to the avenging demon," who inspires further sin just as the spiritual demon inspires ascent toward God (20–21). Hermes asks about the stages of the ascent to God and is told of the seven stages and of the final union with God: "This is the good end for those who possess knowledge: to be deified" (22). Pimander then commands Hermes to use what he has learned to save other men from damnation.

Several important features emerge from this compact myth. First, the cosmogony makes the creation a work of beauty and harmony that is divinely inspired and maintained by celestial influences. The material world is not inherently evil or an inherent threat to man. On the contrary, primal man and nature love each other. Nevertheless, there are aspects of the world that are turned away from divine influence and retain the properties of the *prima materia*, having the tendency to dissolve or to revert to their original state as part of moist/humid nature. The next chapter will show that Ficino develops an elaborate philosophical explanation of the need for celestial influence to flow constantly into the terrestrial world in order to prevent its disintegration. It will also show that he argues that man's highest vocation is that of the magus who can assist in the drawing down of celestial influence in order to arrest the tendency toward disintegration.

In this connection it is important to note man's special creation and his exalted status among the celestial powers. The Supreme God directs the Demiurge to carry out the creation of the world, but God creates man. When he is created, man is shown the beauty of the creation and is encouraged by God to become actively involved in it. Even after man undergoes union with nature and experiences the final stages of his evolution, he retains his capacity for godlike knowledge and creativity.[6]

This cosmogony, then, resolves the tensions that Blumenberg claims early Christianity faced in its effort to explain evil in the world without compromising the majesty of God. God formed a perfect creation, but the material needs constant monitoring and maintenance through celestial influences. The "bad" tendencies are due to matter's inclination to decompose back into its original, unformed condition. Despite this

---

6. This is in contrast to Gnostic myths in which spiritual man loses his divinity as he descends toward the material world.

inclination, the world is a work of beauty and a suitable home for man, especially when he becomes actively involved in it. The explanation of man's loss of immortality makes it clear that matter is not inherently evil. For the man whose life is oriented toward the light (knowledge and God), the world is not a temptation or an obstruction. Only if man has turned from the light is he susceptible to the attraction of the flesh and inclined toward darkness (a material existence). This pursuit of material pleasure is a willful choice; it is not the result of original sin or of the inherent evil in the world. In fact, the myth stands in strong contrast to dualistic views of the tension between the flesh and the spirit, the secular and the sacred.

Another notable feature of the myth is its emphasis on man's capacity for godlike knowledge and on knowledge as the means of salvation. At man's creation God provides him with the knowledge needed to exercise his role as a divine cocreator, and the myth contains repeated references to parallels between the divine *Nous* and man's *nous* and to the role of the *Logos* as the link between man, the creation, and the Supreme God.[7] Man is damned to a material existence only if he willfully ignores or denies the noetic dimension of his soul.

These themes are repeated elsewhere in the *Pimander*. Book 11, for instance, affirms God's shaping influence in the world and asserts that creation is ongoing. That is, creation is not a one-time event and God is not remote from creation. God is always present supplying beauty and order to the creation. In this segment, even deterioration and disintegration are viewed as part of the ongoing creation or divine becoming. "It is by the action of God that all things come into being. Death is not the destruction of the assembled elements in a body, but the breaking of their union. The change is called death because the body dissolves, but I declare to you, my dear Hermes, that the beings who are thus dissolved are but transformed."[8] This same segment urges Hermes to view the world

---

7. The myth, like classical philosophy's concept of the cosmos, emphasizes the link between *Logos* as the source of order and *logos* as man's understanding of the ordering principles of creation.

8. *Corpus Hermeticum,* book 11. The English translation is taken from Frances Yates, *Giordano Bruno and the Hermetic Tradition* (Chicago: University of Chicago Press, 1964), 31-33. Although Yates does not offer complete translations, she does set the materials in an interpretative framework that complements the analysis offered here. An English translation is also found in volume 4 of *Hermetica,* 4 vols., ed. and trans. Walter Scott (1924-1936; reprint, London: Dawsons of Pall Mall, 1968). This translation is not altogether reliable, however, because Scott at times makes freehanded revisions. In the translation of book 1, for example, he apparently finds the text's description of God's love of man as erotic (*eros*) offensive and deletes the phrase.

through the intellect (*nous*) and thereby see its eternity and divinity. Then, in a remarkable passage, Pimander urges Hermes to discover God by recognizing him in everything that exists.

> It is so that you must conceive of God; all that is, he contains within himself like thoughts, the world, himself, the All. Therefore unless you make yourself equal to God, you cannot understand God: for the like is not intelligible save to the like. Make yourself grow to a greatness beyond measure, by a bound free yourself from the body; raise yourself above all time, become Eternity; then you will understand God. Believe that nothing is impossible for you, think yourself immortal and capable of understanding all, all arts, all sciences, the nature of every living being. . . . If you embrace in your thought all things at once, times, places, substances, qualities, quantities, you may understand God.[9]

The twelfth and last book also affirms man's capacity for divinity through the intellect but warns that those who choose not to follow the intellect become animalic. "The intellect, O Tat, is drawn from the very substance of God. In men, this intellect is God; and so some men are gods and their humanity is near to the divinity. When man is not guided by intellect, he falls below himself into an animal state." This passage also underscores man's ability to transcend fate through knowledge to become immortal and godlike. "All men are subject to destiny but those in possession of the word, in whom intellect commands, are not under it in the same manner as others. God's two gifts to man of intellect and the word have the same value as immortality. If man makes right use of these, he differs in no way from the immortals."[10]

The *Asclepius,* which had been translated into Latin already, was regarded by Ficino as the second "divine" work by Hermes Trismegistus. It is, therefore, appropriate to look at some sections of it that complement themes in the *Pimander.* The first is an account of another revelatory experience, in which four spiritualized men invoke the presence of God, who speaks through Hermes. This revelation repeats the theme of God's abiding presence in the cosmos and of the ongoing process of creation.

> All descends from heaven, from the One who is the All, by the intermediary of the heaven. Attend carefully to this, with full application of your divine intellect, for the doctrine of the divinity is like a torrential flood coming down from the heights with violent impetuosity. From the celestial bodies there are spread throughout the world continual effluvia, through the souls of all species and of all individuals from one end to the

---

9. Yates, *Giordano Bruno,* 32.
10. Ibid., 31–33.

other of nature. Matter has been prepared by God to be the receptacle of all forms; and nature, imprinting the forms by means of the four elements, prolongs up to heaven the series of beings.

This same section contains the famous reference to man as the *magnum miraculum*. It occurs as part of a passage emphasizing man's likeness to the gods and explaining his dual nature.

> When God had created the second god, he seemed to him beautiful and he loved him as the offspring of his divinity. . . . But there had to be another being who could contemplate what God had made and so he created man. Seeing that man could not regulate all things unless he gave him a material envelope he gave him a body. Thus man was formed from a double origin, so that he could both admire and adore celestial things and take care of terrestrial things and govern them.[11]

Here we have another positive explanation of man's dual nature. Man's body links him to the material realm just as his intellect links him to the celestial.[12] It is a necessary condition for him to be able to know, understand, and control nature.

This passage is followed by a detailed explanation of the various deities governing the world, and then ensues the well-known and controversial description of man's capacity to make gods.

> Having spoken of the society which unites gods and men [i.e., having discussed the celestial influences], you must know, O Asclepius, the power and force of man. Just as the Lord and Father is the creator of the gods of heaven, so man is the author of the gods who reside in the temples. Not only does he receive life, but he gives it in his turn. Not only does he progress towards God, but he *makes gods*. (37)

These statues, the text continues, are animated statues full of *sensus* and *spiritus*, who can accomplish many things, foretelling the future, giving ills to men and curing them.[13] From the context, it is clear that these images or talismans are the means man uses to draw down the power of the heavens and help in the ongoing creative process. A later passage underscores the use of astral magic by again referring to man as the great miracle and claiming that his most marvelous ability is his ability to make gods.

11. Ibid., 35–36.
12. Recall the earlier passage which contends that there must be a likeness between the knower and the object known. Because the like is not intelligible save to the like, "unless you make yourself equal to God, you cannot understand God" (Yates, *Giordano Bruno*, 31–32).
13. Ibid., 37.

There is one final segment of the *Asclepius* that needs to be introduced into the discussion because it speaks to Blumenberg's emphasis on ancient explanations of the problem of evil in the world. In the texts we have already examined, evil is not inherent in the world and man is not flawed with original sin. Yet the *Asclepius* warns of a time when chaos and despair will fill the world. Egypt, the holy land that Hermes has served as priest-king, will be overrun by barbarians who will destroy the true religion, and the gods will move from earth back to heaven and leave behind only evil angels, who will goad men to commit every conceivable crime. "Then the earth will lose its equilibrium, the sea will no longer be navigable, the heaven will no longer be full of stars. . . . The earth will moulder, the soil will be no longer fertile, the air itself will grow thick with a lugubrious torpor" (39). The lament does not explain the origin of this time of troubles, except to say that it will occur when barbarians, who do not understand the true religion, overrun Egypt. Instead, the purpose of this passage is to provide a reassurance that the condition is only temporary and that God will intervene to renew the world and man.

> Such will be the old age of the world, irreligion, disorder, confusion of all goods. When all these things have come to pass, O Asclepius, then the Lord and Father, the god first in power and the demiurge of the One God, having considered these customs and voluntary crimes, endeavoring by his will, which is the divine will, to bar the way to vices and universal corruption and to correct errors, he will annihilate all malice, either by effacing it in a deluge or by consuming it by fire, or destroying it by pestilential maladies diffused in many places. Then he will bring back the world to its first beauty, so that this world may again be worthy of reverence and admiration, and that God also, creator and restorer of so great a work, may be glorified by the men who shall live then in continual hymns of praise and benedictions. That is what the rebirth of the world will be; a renewal of all good things, a holy and most solemn restoration of Nature herself, imposed by force in the course of time . . . by the will of God.[14]

Ficino, as already noted, found the Hermetic writings parallel to the Mosaic and regarded them as prefiguring the Christian revelation. His commentary on book 1 of the *Pimander,* the "Egyptian Genesis," draws several parallels: Moses describes a darkness over the abyss and the spirit of God brooding over the waters; Hermes sees a darkness and the Word of God warming the Moist Nature. Moses describes creation by

14. Ibid., 39–40.

The Renaissance Revival of the Prisca Theologia

the word of God; Hermes identifies the word with the Logos or Son of God. Both describe man being made in the image of God, both contain a command to the species to be fruitful and multiply, and both explain how we may regain our immortality.[15]

There are, however, significant differences in the two myths, and these are important to note in relation to the issues raised by Blumenberg. The most striking contrast is in the emphasis on knowledge. In two of the Genesis stories, man is punished for his effort to obtain knowledge that would make him like God. The first occurs in the third chapter when mankind is tempted to eat from the Tree of Knowledge (and the Tree of Life). For this sin man is driven from Eden and punished not only with physical suffering, but also by a profound rupture in his union with God. This theme of divine knowledge being forbidden to man is also a central element in the story of the Tower of Babel. In this myth man decides to build a tower that will permit him to storm the heavens and occupy the place of God. To confound man's attempt to overstep his boundaries in such a defiant way, God disrupts his ability to communicate. By contrast, the Hermetic myths underscore man's divinity and describe man as possessing both godlike knowledge and the creative capacity to use that knowledge to emulate God's creation. Rather than denying or forbidding man to possess knowledge that would make him truly like God, the Hermetic myths portray this as man's basic nature and the most precious gift of his Father.

Several other important comparisons should also be made. First, man precedes creation and has a cosmogonic role to play. He is not made by God out of the dust of the earth but is an emanation of God and is of the same substance (*nous*). Second, man is given the magus's dominion over the macrocosm and not just the earth. Third, godlike knowledge is the source of man's salvation; it is not the source of sin. Moreover, the Hermetic ascent up the seven stages toward union with God seems analogous to the effort to build a Tower of Babel.

In light of Blumenberg's emphasis on Gnosticism, it is useful to provide a brief comparison of these Hermetic views with the basic understanding of creation and man's place in the world expressed in the ancient Gnostic materials.[16] This can be accomplished through a brief examination of one of the classic Gnostic texts known as the "Hymn of the Pearl." This text opens as follows:

---

15. *Opera Omnia,* 4:1850.
16. The Hermetic materials, as already noted, are Gnostic in the general sense of emphasizing salvation through knowledge. The contrast developed here is with the pessimistic Gnosticism emphasized by Blumenberg (for instance, that of Marcion).

> When I was a little child and dwelt in the kingdom of my Father's house and delighted in the wealth and splendor of those who raised me, my parents sent me forth from the East, our homeland, with provisions for the journey. From the riches of our treasure-house they tied me a burden: great it was, yet light, so that I might carry it alone. . . . They took off from me the robe of glory which in their love they had made for me, and my purple mantle that was woven to conform exactly to my figure, and made a covenant with me, and wrote it in my heart that I might not forget it: "When thou goest down into Egypt and bringest the One Pearl which lies in the middle of the sea which is encircled by the snorting serpent, thou shalt put on again thy robe of glory and thy mantle over it and with thy brother our next in rank be heir in our kingdom."[17]

The narrator then gives an account of his journey into Egypt. While in Egypt he meets "one of my race" who warns against the Egyptians and "contact with the unclean ones." Despite his precaution, the Egyptians "ingratiated themselves with me, and mixed me [drink] with their cunning, and gave me to taste of their meat; and I forgot that I was a king's son and served their king. I forgot the Pearl for which my parents had sent me. Through the heaviness of their nourishment I sank into deep slumber" (114; translator's brackets).

This "ingratiation" is a trap deliberately sprung on the royal visitor by the Egyptians. The son's predicament causes great anxiety in his father's kingdom, and it is decided that all of the royal governors and officers of the land will prepare a letter and send it to the son.

> From thy father the King of Kings, and from thy mother, mistress of the East, and from thy brother, our next in rank, unto thee, our son in Egypt, greeting. Awake and rise up out of thy sleep, and perceive the words of our letter. Remember that thou art a king's son: behold whom thou hast served in bondage. Be mindful of the Pearl, for whose sake thou hast departed into Egypt. Remember thy robe of glory, recall thy splendid mantle, that thou mayest put them on and deck thyself with them and thy name be read in the book of the heroes and thou become with thy brother, our deputy, heir in our kingdom. (114)

The message is given over to an eagle who is capable of avoiding "the children of Babel and the rebellious demons of Sarbûg." Upon receipt of the message, the son remembers his royal origin and awakens from the

---

17. The translation is found in Hans Jonas, *The Gnostic Religion: The Message of the Alien God and the Beginnings of Christianity*, 2d. ed. (Boston: Beacon, 1963), 113–14. Subsequent quotations are cited with page numbers in the text. This treatment closely parallels that found in my *Sacralizing the Secular: The Renaissance Origins of Modernity* (Baton Rouge: Louisiana State University Press, 1989), 46–48.

slumber that he had fallen into. Immediately he sets out "to enchant the terrible and snorting serpent," recover the pearl, and return home to his father's kingdom. "Their filthy and impure garment I put off, and left it behind in their land, and directed my way that I might come to the light of our homeland, the East" (114–15). Upon return, his mission accomplished, there is much joy that the pearl is returned and that the son is safely home.

Even without being familiar with the specific Gnostic meaning of certain symbols, the thrust of this myth is clear and its contrast to the Hermetic myths evident. The King of Kings is, of course, the supreme God. The son who is sent forth is the Son of God and is comparable to primal man in the Hermetic myth. In attempting to recover the pearl, he becomes trapped in matter and forgets his divine origin and mission. The pessimistic, dualistic view of the physical is expressed in the trickery involving food and drink, in the filthiness of the garments worn to be like the Egyptians, and in the slumber and sleepwalking as consequences of treachery. The eagle is a universal symbol of a divine messenger. The symbolism of the pearl is not so readily apparent, though myths of a great treasure lost in the dross of the world are a frequent component of dualistic religions and most often refer to the soul that becomes imprisoned in matter and has to be rescued by divine action. Without explaining how the divine soul becomes entrapped, the myth, nevertheless, expresses this as the fundamental condition. The effects of the material world are so strong that even God's son forgets his true nature and his real home.

This hymn is regarded as Gnostic because of its emphasis on knowledge (*gnosis*) as the means of salvation (regaining one's divine station). This feature is also found, however, in the Hermetic myths' doctrine that knowledge enables man to achieve his fulfillment as the Son of God. Fundamental differences exist, however, in the two views of what constitutes salvation through knowledge. In the Gnostic myth salvation depends on escaping from the world. In Hermetic myth the world is necessary for mankind to exercise his divine creativity, and it is in the world that man creates the social microcosm that completes creation. Hence, knowledge of the world is a form of spiritual disease (*agnoia*) for Gnosticism, but in Hermetic myth knowledge (*logos*) of the world is God-given and is the key to man's power over nature, and this power over nature is what makes man godlike.

Given its fundamental doctrines of the world as a prison and of *gnosis* as the knowledge that produces salvation through liberation from the physical world, it is difficult to understand how Gnostic myths can be aligned with modern progress and self-assertion. On the other hand, the

Hermetic myths and symbols have a close correspondence to modern dreams of inner-worldly fulfillment. The Hermetic materials present man as magus. The magus possesses the knowledge and has God's approval to work within the natural order to perfect it and to make his unique, creative contribution through the installation of the microcosmic order of society.

The Hermetic doctrine, then, offers an important alternative resolution to the theological and cosmological problems that Blumenberg maintains Christianity faced. It shares with Gnosticism the central doctrine of knowledge as the means of salvation, but it does not share Gnosticism's negative views of creation. In fact, it preserves the positive view of the cosmos. At the same time, it places more emphasis on God's active role in creation. True, the Supreme God utilizes subordinate deities, but he is in ultimate control. The bad or evil in the natural world is the result of the tendency of material things to disintegrate, to revert to their original, inert, natural condition. But this tendency is counterbalanced by God's continual renewal of creation, which can be enhanced by the magus's efforts to remedy the "bad" in the natural world. It is also important to note that the Hermetic materials do not place the blame for evil on a primordial flaw in man. Men are free to follow the guide of reason or free to submerge themselves in material existence. Each individual makes that decision.

Blumenberg's failure to consider this tradition in either his discussion of the Hellenistic period or the early modern period might create the impression that it was of marginal consequence. Eugenio Garin and others, however, have shown that Ficino's *Pimander* was widely circulated and frequently reprinted. Moreover, other major figures in the fifteenth and sixteenth centuries drew upon the Hermetic doctrines and, like Ficino, explored their significance for issues in theology.[18]

One of the most important consequences of this renewed interest in the *prisca theologia* was the new emphasis given to magic. Ficino, Pico, Agrippa, and Bruno all recognized the connection between the *prisca theologia* and the *prisca magia*, the occult knowledge system that allowed man to control nature and perfect society. As a result, magic, which was condemned by medieval theology, became the highest stage of philosophy and inspired the search for the means to control nature and to perfect society. Chapters 6 and 7 will show that this search inspired Agrippa, Bruno, and Bacon with a holistic vision of combining scientific,

---

18. See, for example, Eugenio Garin, *Medioevo e Rinascimento: Studi e ricerche* (Rome: Laterza, 1987), 274–79.

and modifies the works of lower nature," to the highest levels, in which man's majesty is demonstrated by his self-governance: "The force of man is almost similar to the divine nature since man by himself, that is through his intelligence and skill, governs himself without being in the least limited by his physical nature and imitates the individual works of the higher nature."[4] To support this contention, Ficino points out that man is more self-sufficient than other animals in meeting his basic needs: ". . . he is endowed by nature with fewer natural aids to bodily protection than the animals, but he himself provides his own supply of food, clothing, bedding, housing, furnishings and arms." Beyond his capacity to meet his physical needs, man is capable of creating "an indescribable variety of pleasures . . . for delighting the five senses." Even more significant, the cogitative reason proves "its own inventive genius . . . through various silk and woollen textiles, paintings, sculptures and buildings." The development of the industrial arts is one of man's most significant achievements because it shows "how man everywhere utilises all the materials of the universe as though all were subject to man."[5] Man's real genius, then, is found in his ability to transform the elements provided by nature to fit his creative purpose.

For Ficino the mastery of fire is a great civilizational act not only because it satisfies physical needs, but much more importantly because of its testimony to man's heavenly nature: "only a celestial animal is delighted by a celestial element." Man's ability to use his "supercelestial intelligence" leads to truly marvelous accomplishments.

> How stupendous the structures of buildings and cities. How ingenious his works of irrigation. He acts as the vicar of God, since he inhabits all the elements and cultivates all, and present on earth, he is not absent from the ether. Indeed he employs not only the elements but all the animals of the elements, terrestrial, aquatic, and flying, for food, comfort and pleasure, and the supernal and celestial ones for learning and the miracles of magic. He not only uses the animals but he rules them. . . . He does not only rule the animals cruelly, but he also governs, fosters and teaches them. Universal providence is proper to God who is the universal cause. Therefore man who universally provides for all things living and not living is a certain god. He is the god without doubt of the animals since he uses all of them, rules them, and teaches some of them. He is established also as god of the elements since he inhabits and cultivates them all. He is, finally, the god of all materials since he handles all, and turns and changes them.

---

4. Trinkaus, 2:482–83/Marcel, 2:224.
5. Trinkaus, 2:483/Marcel, 2:224–26.

Anyone who dominates the body in so many and such great things and acts as the vicar of immortal God is without doubt immortal.[6]

This is one of the grandest hymns to man's genius in all of Renaissance literature. Still, Ficino has not reached the height of his praise for the terrestrial god *Anthropos*. Man's self-governance and his most godlike acts are at the zenith when he recreates the heavenly kingdom on earth.

> . . . the arts of this type, although they mould the matter of the universe and command the animals, and thus imitate God, the creator of nature, are nevertheless inferior to those arts which imitating the heavenly kingdom undertake the responsibility of human government. . . . [M]an alone so abounds in perfection that he rules himself first, which no beasts do, then governs his family, administers the state, rules peoples and commands the entire world.

The ignorant or the ill-informed may assume that man's efforts and achievements in the world are directed toward the present life and the attainment of satisfaction within it, but according to Ficino the effect is just the opposite. Intellectual achievement exhausts the body.[7]

> . . . the arts of this sort . . . [imitate] divine providence. . . . The subtle computation of numbers, the meticulous description of figures, the most obscure movement of lines, the mysterious consonance of music, long observation of the stars, the study of natural causes, the investigation of enduring things, the eloquence of orators, the madness of poets—in all of these the soul of man despises the ministry of the body as though he one day would be able and now already begins to live without the aid of the body.

This crucial passage implies that the immortality of man actually begins in this life through the mastery of the body and the subjugation of the natural, the celestial, and the supercelestial influences. In these achievements, Ficino says that man "is endowed with a genius, as I would put it, that is almost the same as that of the Author of the heavens, and that *man would be able to make the heavens in some way if he only possessed the instruments and the celestial material,* since he does make them now, although out of other material, yet very similar in structure."[8]

The position that Ficino is taking is truly extraordinary even by Renaissance standards. In the biblical stories of creation, man is twice punished for attempting to gain the knowledge and the power to be like God.

---

6. Trinkaus, 2:483–84/ Marcel, 2:224–26.
7. Trinkaus, 2:484/ Marcel, 2:224–26.
8. Trinkaus, 2:484–85/ Marcel, 2:224–26; my italics.

Ficino, on the other hand, maintains that man's comprehension of the world is so completely comparable to God's that he could make the heavens if he only possessed the instruments and the celestial material.

> ... the mind in comprehending conceives of as many things in itself as God in knowing makes in the world. By speaking it expresses as many into the air; with a reed it writes as many on paper. By making it constructs as many in the material of the world. Therefore he would be proven mad who would deny that the soul, which in the arts and in governing competes with God, is divine.[9]

This ability to emulate God even extends to the capacity to work miracles:

> The human mind vindicates to itself a right to divinity not only in forming and shaping matter through the methods of arts, as we have said, but also in transmuting the species of things by command, which work is indeed called a miracle. . . . Here we marvel that the souls of men dedicated to God rule the elements, call upon the winds, force the clouds to rain, chase away fogs, cure the diseases of human bodies and the rest. These plainly were done in certain ages among various peoples, as poets sing, historians narrate, and those who are the most excellent of philosophers, especially the Platonists, do not deny, the ancient theologians testify, above all Hermes and Orpheus, and the later theologians also prove by word and deed.[10]

Here we have arrived at the core of Ficino's new understanding of human nature: "The entire striving of our soul is that it become God. Such striving is no less natural to men than the effort of flight is to birds."[11] This yearning, which is stronger and more persistent than any appetite, is placed in us by God: "For who but God, Himself, whom we seek, would have inserted this into our souls? who, since He alone is the author of the species, inserts a proper appetite into the species."[12]

To explain man's capacity for divinization, Ficino explains that man is unique because he has a potential that no other being has, not even the angels. Man's soul is a microcosm and man may become the lowest of creatures or the highest creator.

---

9. Trinkaus, 2:486/ Marcel, 2:228–29. The phrase "est aemula Dei," which Trinkaus translates "competes with God," should perhaps be rendered "strives to equal God," given the basic meaning of *aemulare*.
10. Trinkaus, 2:486/ Marcel, 2:229 (book 13, chapter 4).
11. "Totus igitur animae nostrae conatus est, ut Deus efficiatur. Conatus talis naturalis est hominibus non minus quam conatus avibus ad volandum." Trinkaus, 487/ Marcel, 247.
12. Trinkaus, 487/ Marcel, 247.

> Man leads the life of a plant in so far as in eating he indulges the body, the life of an animal when he flatters his senses, the life of a man in so far as he consults reason in human affairs, the life of heroes as he investigates natural phenomena, the life of demons when he engages in mathematical speculation, the life of angels according as he inquires into divine mysteries, the life of God as far as he does all for the sake of God. The soul of every man experiences all these things in a certain way in himself, although each in his own way, and so mankind strives to become all beings since it leads the lives of all beings.[13]

By what instrument and process does man move through the "totality of being?" The answer is that the mind in knowing something becomes the thing it knows.

The root of this notion is found in the passages in the *Pimander* and the *Asclepius* which assert that knowledge depends on likeness or similarity between the knower and the known. Anything completely unlike or alien to the knower is incomprehensible. Ficino employs this principle to support his argument that man knows the world through his participation in it and knows God because of man's likeness to him. He then contends that man's discovery of his own ability to know the world and recreate it demonstrates that he shares two of God's primary attributes: comprehensive knowledge and creativity.

Man's mastery of the natural world may at first appear to be directed toward the satisfaction of physical needs and desires, but the desire to dominate is not limited to the empires of the world.

> But in what pertains to the desire for victory, the immense magnificence of our soul may manifestly be seen from this, that he will not be satisfied with the empire of this world, if, having conquered this one, he learns that there remains another world which he has not yet subjugated. . . . Thus man wishes no superior and no equal and will not permit anything to be left out and excluded from his rule. This status belongs to God alone. Therefore he seeks a divine condition.[14]

If we now review Ficino's "new understanding" we find six principal elements:

1. The yearning to be like God, implanted in us by God, is the strongest of human drives and motivation.

2. To be like God means being free of control or domination by any force or factor.

3. Self-control or governance is acquired through knowledge. The

---

13. Trinkaus, 490/Marcel, 256.
14. Book 14, chapter 4; Trinkaus, 491/Marcel, 260.

ignorant can only participate in the lower levels of existence; the wise man uses his participation as a means of knowing and mastering the lower orders and conditions of life.

4. Only man has the ability to dominate the created order and alter his fate.

5. Knowledgeable participation in the world is man's means of self-divinization. Man demonstrates his godlike knowledge and creativity through his mastery of the world.

6. Man's physical attachment to the world is not a threat to man's immortality; in fact, his dominion as a terrestrial god is the beginning of his union with God and his gaining of immortality.

Ficino's description of man as a terrestrial god shows that he has drawn heavily from the Hermetic materials and has introduced into early modern thought concepts identical to those Blumenberg identifies as characteristically modern. In the *De vita triplici,* Ficino also emphasizes man's ability to dominate nature and argues that the wisest philosopher-theologian and the true master of the cosmos is the magus.

De Vita Triplici

De vita triplici is a crucial text for understanding the Renaissance cosmology and the elevation of magic to the highest form of philosophy. Until recently, however, its "pseudo-scientific" medical prescriptions and its astral magic were regarded as an embarrassing remnant of medieval superstition that modern science and reason eventually displace. Two early studies that helped to call attention to the importance of this text for understanding the development of the fundamental Renaissance themes of human dignity and creativity are Klibansky, Panofsky, and Saxl's *Saturn and Melancholy* and Walker's *Spiritual and Demonic Magic.*[15]

Saturn and Melancholy explores changes in the intellectual climate that support the Renaissance celebration of human dignity, individuality, creativity, and self-governance. Medieval medicine and astrology regarded Saturn as both the source of genius and the debilitating effects of melancholy, the "scholar's malady." Ficino's *De vita triplici* is extraordi-

---

15. R. Klibansky, E. Panofsky, and F. Saxl, *Saturn and Melancholy: Studies in the History of Natural Philosophy, Religion and Art* (New York: Basic Books, 1964); D. P. Walker, *Spiritual and Demonic Magic from Ficino to Campanella* (1958; reprint, South Bend, Ind.: University of Notre Dame Press, 1975).

nary in maintaining that it is possible to use astral magic to intensify the benefits of Saturn and, at the same time, to arrest its detrimental side effects. The result of this magical manipulation of celestial influences is that the magician is able to heighten his intellectual abilities and avoid the disturbing influences of melancholy. For Klibansky et al. this marks a fundamental turning point in Renaissance and modern thought because it portrays man as the master of his destiny, manipulating the forces governing the natural world to create an ideal environment for the exercise of his genius. Although this book clearly opens new perspectives on the climate of Renaissance ideas, it should be noted that it seeks to separate the desirable traits (self-governance, for example) from their origins in Ficino's astral magic. The study that establishes magic as a central rather than a peripheral element in Neoplatonic thought is Walker's *Spiritual and Demonic Magic*. This work demonstrates the importance of the *prisca theologia* for Ficino and other early modern figures through convincing textual references to Orphic hymn-singing, Pythagorean numerology, and Hermetic magic.

The purpose of the analysis of the *De vita* offered here is to connect its emphasis on astral magic to the "new understanding of human nature" developed in the *Theologia Platonica*. The portion of the *De vita* that will receive detailed examination is the third book, but it is necessary to prepare for this discussion by briefly summarizing the contents of the first two books. The specific thread that we want to follow is Ficino's argument that astral magic is simply the highest form of natural medicine. Ficino sets the stage for this argument by demonstrating that therapeutic medicine depends upon knowledge of planetary powers immanent in physical substances so that all medicine is natural magic.

In his preface, Ficino explains that *De vita triplici* is a medical treatise that is intended as a complement to his philosophical work. In his previous writings, he has sought to be a physician of the soul; in these three books he aims to minister to the general health and well-being of intellectuals, who often neglect the physical in pursuit of the spiritual. The text then sets for itself three interrelated tasks: (1) the analysis of the adverse physiological conditions created through rigorous mental activity and the prescription for balancing these deleterious effects, (2) the description of ways in which the philosopher can prolong his life in order to have sufficient time to complete his quest, and (3) a comprehensive explanation of the use of talismans and other means of drawing down the benefits of celestial influences and putting them in service to the philosopher/magus.

In the first chapter of book 1, Ficino explains that he is offering help that scholars have never had available before. Although scholars have long recognized the availability of guides who can lead the way on the "long journey which barely, at the last, by continual hardship leads through to the high temple of the nine Muses," there has not been until now a doctor "who might reach a hand to them as they go, and help with salutary counsels and medicines," aiding "young people and mature people enervated by too fierce pursuit of Minerva!"[16] Athletes, artists, and craftsmen have long known the skills necessary to take care of the tools and resources on which their art depends, but "only the priests of the Muses, only the hunters after the highest good and truth, are so negligent (oh shame!) and so unfortunate, that they seem wholly to neglect that instrument with which they are able in a way to measure and grasp the whole world" (111). This instrument, Ficino explains, is the *spiritus* itself, which doctors define as some vapor of the blood—pure, subtle, warm, and clear. In subsequent chapters Ficino explains the physiology that leads to the health problems of scholars. In chapter 3 he cautions that men of letters should be very diligent in caring for their limbs, powers, and spirit; and they should be particularly careful to avoid phlegm and black bile. "Phlegm dulls and suffocates the intelligence, while melancholy [black bile], if it is too abundant or vehement, vexes the mind with continual care and frequent absurdities and unsettles the judgment" (113).

In chapters 4 and 5 Ficino explains that there are three sets of causes for melancholia in scholars: the first is astrological, the second is natural (due to the physiology of the body), and the third is human. Philosophers are particularly susceptible to melancholia because contemplation of the eternal has an adverse physiological effect on the body. The remainder of book 1 is devoted to a discussion of steps to counter these various sets of adverse influences. All of these prescriptions are astrological. Following the general astrological schema is a more narrowly defined series of medical practices for treating stomach disorders, insomnia, and other physical maladies.

In the concluding chapter of book 1, Ficino exhorts scholars to take care of their bodily spirit because it is important to their search for truth; but "they must try still harder to cultivate with the teachings of moral philosophy the incorporeal spirit, i.e., the intellect, by which alone truth, being itself incorporeal, is apprehended. For it is wrong to cherish only the slave of the soul, the body, and to neglect the soul, the lord and ruler

---

16. *Three Books on Life: A Critical Edition and Translation with Introduction and Notes*, vol. 57 of Medieval and Renaissance Texts and Studies, ed. Carol Kaske and John Clark (Binghamton, N.Y.: Renaissance Society of America, 1989), 109. Subsequent quotations from *De vita triplici* are also taken from this edition and are cited with page numbers in the text.

of the body . . ." (161). This passage is not so much a conclusion of the previous treatise as it is a transition to the next dimension of Ficino's therapeutic program—steps to be taken to care for the soul.

Book 2 opens with the assertion that a long life is necessary if scholars are to perfect their knowledge. Unfortunately, however, long life is not something the philosopher is given by fate. In fact, the opposite is the case: his intellectual efforts create disturbances in the body. Fortunately, however, man is not like other beings; he is able to alter the conditions of his life. Ficino argues that

> a long life is not just something the fates promise once for all from the beginning, but something that is procured by our effort. This is both acknowledged by astrologers, when they deal with elections and images, and confirmed by the careful concern and the experience of physicians. Through this foresight not only do people who are strong by nature very often attain a long life but also sometimes the weakest. . . . (167)

Ficino then cites the *prisca theologia*'s accounts of those who were weak in body but through the powers of their soul and mind were able to prolong their life. Beginning in chapter 12, the prophylactic measures for enhancing life broaden to include the choice of an appropriate place to live, and chapter 13 initiates a discussion of how the planets can be useful in old age. In both cases the benefit is accomplished by utilizing organic materials containing concentrations of desirable planetary influences. Ficino lists some plants, herbs, and other materials (for instance, "Jupiter, [will help with] pistachio-nuts and raisins; Venus, hepatica, endive, slag, and chicory"; 203) and then explains how these material things contain the benefit of celestial influences. After explaining the benefit of Venus that is derived from green things, Ficino elaborates in chapter 14:

> For since these most beautiful and almost celestial things could not be created under the earth without the greatest gift from the heavens, it is probable that in things of this kind wonderful powers from the heavens inhere. A compound of this kind—which in dilating and illuminating the spirit equally collects it—so delights it inwardly and refreshes it as greenness does externally to the eyes. . . . (207)

Book 3 is concerned with drawing the benefits of planetary influence. Chapter 1 opens with a description of the world soul (*anima mundi*) as the macrocosmic link between divine intellect and the material world and is reminiscent of the discussion in the *Theologia Platonica* of the human soul as the mediating force between the mind and the body.

> If there were only these two things in the universe—on one side the Intellect, on the other the Body—but no Soul, then neither would the Intellect

be attracted to the Body (for Intellect is absolutely motionless, without affect, which is the principle of motion, and very far away from the Body), nor would the Body be drawn to the Intellect (for Body is in itself powerless, unsuited for motion, and far removed from the Intellect). But if a Soul which conforms to both were placed between them, an attraction will easily occur to each one on either side. . . . In her own fashion she contains all things and is proportionally [Intellect: Soul:: Soul: Body] near to both. Therefore she is equally connected with everything, even with those things which are at a distance from one other, because they are not at a distance from her. For besides the fact that on the one side she conforms to the divine and on the other side to the transient, and even turns to each by desire, at the same time she is wholly and simultaneously everywhere. (243; translator's brackets)

The second paragraph contains a key passage, though Ficino does not take much pain to explain it or to establish its central importance.

In addition, the World-soul possesses by divine power precisely as many seminal reasons of things as there are Ideas in the Divine Mind. By these seminal reasons she fashions the same number of species in matter. That is why every single species corresponds through its own seminal reason to its own Idea and oftentimes through this reason it can easily receive something from the Idea—since indeed it was made through the reason from the Idea. This is why, if at any time the species degenerates from its proper form, it can be formed again with the reason as the proximate intermediary and, through the Idea as intermediary, can then be easily reformed. (243)

In this last sentence Ficino indicates that the degeneration and disintegration occurring in "fallen nature" can be overcome by using the world soul to draw the material thing back into conformity with its eternal form or idea. The significance of this passage will be examined in detail below.

The next important development is the introduction of the world spirit (*spiritus mundi*).[17] While the soul is the link between the eternal form and fallen nature, the agent for ongoing interaction is the *spiritus mundi*.

. . . just as the power of our soul is brought to bear on our members through the spirit, so the force of the World-soul is spread under the

---

17. Ficino never provides a concise definition of the *spiritus*. Its function emerges from his discussion of the world soul and its analogous role to that of the human soul. The world soul (*anima mundi*) is the locus of the union of divine form and matter. The instrument of this union and its preservation is the *spiritus mundi*.

World-soul through all things through the quintessence, which is active everywhere, as the spirit inside the World's Body, but that this power is instilled especially into those things which have absorbed the most of this kind of spirit. (247)

The *spiritus mundi*, though permeating the whole world, is concentrated in certain things, and by manipulation of them it is possible for our own souls to draw into themselves the benefits of the world spirit.[18]

In chapter 2 Ficino contends that the Platonists and the astrologers agree that

> by an application of our spirit to the spirit of the cosmos, achieved by physical science and our affect, celestial goods pass to our soul and body. This happens from down here through our spirit within us which is a mediator, strengthened then by the spirit of the cosmos, and from above by way of the rays of the stars acting favorably on our spirit, which not only is similar to the rays by nature but also then makes itself more like celestial things. (255)

He then offers a lengthy description of the range of planetary benefits that are useful to the scholar not only for the maintenance of the body but also for the cultivation of the soul and the powers of the mind.[19] He ends chapter 8, however, with a cautious note. In the last paragraph Ficino quotes the ancient theologians to the effect that the world spirit is capable of action not only on the body but on the intellect as well (because it is a mediating agent between the two). At this point, Ficino realizes that he is entering into controversial areas at best and, more probably, into a conflict with Christian orthodox belief. He therefore prudently adds that our knowledge is not perhaps certain enough to understand how these various effects are rendered. It is not clear how they work, but it is evident that they do work. Moreover, his own interest in and use of these celestial powers are restricted to things that are within the realm of natural philosophy and therefore consistent with orthodox theology. Ficino then moves to a discussion of the "natural" influence of the planets and how their benefits might be cultivated.

Chapter 11 opens with an important summary of the line of argument that leads from book 1 to book 3.

---

18. Ficino explains that the fifth essence, the *spiritus mundi*, can be absorbed by us if we know how to separate it from the other elements with which it is heavily mixed, or at least if we know how to use those things that contain it. This is especially true of things in which it is pure, such as select wines and sugars, balsam, gold, and precious stones. See Kaske and Clark, 247.

19. These subjects are treated throughout the remainder of book 3, but see especially chapters 11 and 22.

Ficino and the Prisca Theologia Tradition

> All these discussions are for this purpose, that through the rays of the stars opportunely received, our spirit properly prepared and purged through natural things may receive the most from the very spirit of the life of the world. The life of the world, innate in everything, is clearly propagated into plants and trees, like the body-hair and tresses of its body. Moreover, the world is pregnant with stones and metals, like its bones and teeth. It sprouts also in shells which live clinging to the earth and to stones. . . .
>
> Likewise by a frequent use of plants and a similar use of living things, you can draw the most from the spirit of the world, especially if you nourish and foster yourself by things which are still living, fresh, and all but still clinging, as it were, to mother earth. . . . (289, 291)

There then follows a description of the organic connections between the material and the planet or star having a desirable effect on human life.

Chapter 13 takes up the most controversial element of Ficino's astral magic, the making of images or talismans. This is handled gingerly and, as Ficino says, is basically a representation of the descriptions contained in the ancient wisdom tradition. Toward the end of chapter 15, Ficino offers his own tentative comment.

> I also often doubt it, and, were it not that all antiquity and all astrologers think they [images or talismans] have a wonderful power, I would deny it. Of course I would not deny it categorically, for I am of the opinion, unless someone should persuade me otherwise, that especially by reason of the material selected they have at least some power towards good health, even though I think much more of it resides in drugs and unguents compounded with the favor of the stars. (321)

He then adds that his purpose in giving this account is only to inform and not necessarily to recommend, though the talismans are part of the revered ancient writings. This is a prudent statement in light of its unorthodox nature, but it is not altogether genuine and heartfelt. Ficino admits that these images work if for no other reason than that the materials themselves contain celestial properties. Furthermore, he adds that this practice is legitimate if it is carried out with the art of the doctor—by following the theory and practice being offered by Ficino rather than being drawn into the realm of unorthodox spiritual or demonic magic. Chapter 18 again discusses the use of images. After giving a brief account from the ancient tradition of the efficacy of these images, he nevertheless cautions that they have an ambiguous history and seem to have been used for as much evil as for good. Again, however, the effect of his argument is to create the impression that these images, used as God intended them, are an aide to man.

In chapter 19 Ficino discusses the construction of a holistic or universal image that could be used to develop sympathetic links between the celestial influences and the material world. Ficino begins chapter 20 by indicating that there are certain natural substances which are so potent with the benefits of the world spirit that through them it is possible to rejuvenate both the body and the soul so that the recipient seems almost reborn. He adds that astrologers have contended that propitious images had a similar power through which they could alter the nature and habits of someone who wears them. They "restore him to a better state, so that he becomes now almost another person; or at least preserve him in good health for a very long time" (351). This discussion is augmented in chapter 21 by a consideration of the analogies of images—words, songs, and music—as ways of tapping directly into celestial influences. Chapter 22 catalogues the sympathetic links between the natural world and the celestial and supercelestial powers. Because it is of central importance, it will be quoted at length.

> Since the heavens have been constructed according to a harmonic plan and move harmonically and bring everything about by harmonic sounds and motions, it is logical that through harmony alone not only human beings but all things below are prepared to receive, according to their abilities, celestial things. In the preceding chapter we distributed the harmony capable of receiving things above into seven steps: through images (as they believe) put together harmonically, through medicines tempered with a certain proper consonance, through vapors and odors completed with similar consonance, through musical songs and sounds (with which rank and power we wish to associate gestures of the body, dancing, and ritual movements), through well-accorded concepts and motions of the imagination, through fitting discourses of reason, through tranquil contemplations of the mind. For just as we expose the body seasonably to the light and heat of the Sun through its daily harmony, that is, through its location, posture, and shape, so also we expose our spirit in order to obtain the occult forces of the stars through a similar harmony of its own, obtained by images, as they believe, certainly by medicines, and by odors harmonically composed. Finally, we expose our soul and our body to such occult forces through the spirit so prepared for things above (as I have often said)—yes, our soul, insofar as it is inclined by its affection to the spirit and body. . . . Similarly, our reason (either through the imagination and the spirit together, or through deliberation, or through both) by imitation is so able to adapt itself to Jupiter. . . . Lastly, the contemplating intellect—insofar as it separates itself not only from things we perceive but even from those things which we commonly imagine and which we prove about human behavior and insofar as it recollects itself in emotion, in intention, and in life to supra-physical things—exposes itself somewhat to Saturn. (363, 365)

This exposure to Saturn, which is injurious to common people, has a beneficial effect on the intellectual person, especially when Saturn is

Ficino and the Prisca Theologia Tradition

brought into conjunction with lunar benefits. Further on, Ficino describes the planetary scheme that is most beneficial to the philosopher/ magus. He then adds:

> The Chaldeans, Egyptians, and Platonists think that by this method one can avoid the malice of fate. For since they believe the celestials are not empty bodies, but bodies divinely animated and ruled moreover by divine Intelligences, no wonder they believe that as many good things as possible come forth from thence for men, goods pertaining not only to our body and spirit but also overflowing somewhat into our soul, and not into our soul from their bodies but from their souls. And they believe too that the same sort of things and more of them flow out from those Intelligences which are above the heavens. (367)

Through a concerted use of the natural influences resident in the material world and through the evocation of celestial powers by spiritual magic, we overcome fate. Chapter 22 concludes:

> Finally, whenever we say "celestial goods descend to us," understand: (1) that gifts from the celestial *bodies* come into our *bodies* through our rightly-prepared spirit. . . . In summary, consider that those who by prayer, by study, by manner of life, and by conduct imitate the beneficence, action, and order of the celestials, since they are more similar to the gods, receive fuller gifts from them. (369)

Chapters 25 and 26, the final two chapters, summarize Ficino's basic argument and attempt to show that his magical practices fall within the natural order of things and are therefore condoned by the Church.

In chapter 26 he repeats his cosmological view of the intimate relation of divine form to the substance of the earth through the soul and the order of the cosmos and its link to the transcendent as part of nature. He uses several examples to show how drawing the benefits of the stars occurs in the most elemental and "natural" parts of life.

> With this in mind, Agriculture prepares the field and the seed for celestial gifts and by grafting prolongs the life of the shoot and refashions it into another and better species. The doctor, the natural philosopher, and the surgeon achieve similar effects in our bodies in order both to strengthen our own nature and to obtain more productively the nature of the universe. The philosopher who knows about natural objects and stars, whom we rightly are accustomed to call a Magus, does the very same things: he seasonably introduces the celestial into the earthly by particular lures just as the farmer interested in grafting brings the fresh graft into the old stock. (387)

To support this view, Ficino invokes ancient authority. According to these passages, the magus's creative powers are like the farmer's. Both are capable of improving existing species and creating new ones. This passage is followed by a discussion of accounts in which the *prisci theologi* had drawn celestial powers into statues, a feat that some Church fathers attributed to unorthodox demonic magic. Ficino, however, maintains that the same effects could be accomplished through acceptable spiritual magic using the world soul as the agent. Here we have reached one of the crucial new dimensions of Ficino's magic. Through a cautious, indirect approach, Ficino develops the argument that benefits derive from the celestial powers through the world spirit and that knowledge of how these influences can be used in medicine and in other prophylactic programs is a gift from God, not a trafficking in demonic practices (though he leaves open the likelihood that ignorant or ill-informed men do end up invoking demonic powers). A fundamental component in the development of his case is his effort to cast the deeds of the *prisci theologi*, whom he is following, into the wholesome realm of spiritual magic derived from the world soul.

> But now let us get back to Hermes, or rather to Plotinus. Hermes says that the priests received an appropriate power from the nature of the cosmos and mixed it. . . . Plotinus follows him and thinks that everything can be easily accomplished by the intermediation of the Anima Mundi, since the Anima Mundi generates and moves the forms of natural things through certain seminal reasons implanted in her from the divine. (391)

Another significant part of Ficino's reformation of magic is his redefinition of medicine and all other improvements in life as *natural* magic—whether it is the work of the physician, the farmer, or the magician. "Nature," says Ficino, "is in all things a magician." Ficino develops this argument by first showing that accepted medical techniques involving diet and other regulatory practices derive their effectiveness from the stars. This is accomplished through utilization of the world spirit, which links divine ideas with the world substance. Medicine is therefore the practical knowledge of planetary influences resident in natural substances. Having established this fundamental notion, Ficino broadens his application to prolonging life in book 2 and to ministering to the soul and the mind in book 3. These measures can be taken because the *spiritus* is resident in the soul and is able through it to affect the intelligence.

This extended discussion of medicine's relation to magic is vital to the reformulation that Ficino wishes to accomplish. His primary aim is to establish an analogy between the physician's knowledge of well-being in the body and the magus's knowledge of the needs of the soul and intellect. Moreover, Ficino intends to move his magic away from the proscriptions against trafficking with demons by maintaining that his magic draws upon the *spiritus mundi* and is therefore *natural* and acceptable to the Church. Ficino reenforces this claim by developing the analogy between the craft of the farmer and the magus. Both draw upon natural forces to improve and to change the physical world for the benefit of man.

The overall result of Ficino's reformulation of magic is precisely as Klibanski et al. describe it in *Saturn and Melancholy*. It provides the epistemological foundation for a new image of man as the master of the natural world and the shaper of his own destiny. Consequently, it is an essential element of Ficino's description of man as a terrestrial god. Also underlying the "new understanding of human nature" is a fundamental reconceptualization of God, the world, and society.

This new view has striking parallels to Blumenberg's description of the features of modernity. Modern man sees his role as the active reshaping of the natural and social worlds. Rather than standing as a passive observer, man must acquire knowledge and use it. Knowledge is not the acquisition of truths that set boundaries or confine man to attunement with what already exists. Knowledge is knowledge of transformation. Of course, there are differences. For Blumenberg man's self-emancipation comes as a result of the retreat of God from the world. In this tradition God is the source, the reason that man can know the world and the powers that govern it. The next three chapters trace parallels between Renaissance thought, science, and the doctrine of progress and will show that the *prisca theologia* tradition directly shapes the root notions of modernity. The first step will be to demonstrate the pervasive influences of the Neoplatonic/Hermetic view of man and nature in the Renaissance; the next step will be to relate it to the elements of the scientific tradition that made science the key to social reformation and progress.

4. Christian and Neoplatonic Themes in Renaissance Art

*T*he previous chapter showed how Ficino drew upon the myths and symbols of the *prisca theologia* to develop an immanentist construction of the soul's relation to the macrocosm. Ficino was drawn to these materials because they were regarded as God's revelations to non-Christian wisemen and therefore could supplement and help to clarify elements of the Christian tradition. In the *Theologia Platonica,* Ficino uses the materials to offer a new understanding of man which describes the tripartite nature of the soul and explains the sources of man's enduring happiness. In *De vita triplici,* Ficino draws upon the Ancient Wisdom to establish parallels between the micro- and macrocosm and argues that God intended for man to be able to manipulate astral influences to improve the human condition.

This chapter will look more closely at orthodox religious views prevalent in the Renaissance that would be compatible with and receptive to the immanentist elements of the Ancient Wisdom revived by Ficino and the Platonic Academy. Obviously, this form of Christian theology would have to be different from the radical dualism that Blumenberg argues comes to dominate and ultimately exhaust late medieval Christianity. The argument offered here is that there is a vital Christian theology that spans from the mid-fourteenth to the mid-sixteenth century and contributes to the Renaissance emphasis on the dignity of man and the goodness of creation. To demonstrate that this was a prominent, influential view, this chapter will analyze the iconographic programs of two of the most important Renaissance artists, Giotto (1266–1337) and Michelangelo (1475–1564). Giotto is generally regarded as the first great artist of the Renaissance, and he is credited with a distinctive new emphasis on individuality and naturalism that shapes the Renaissance imagination for the next two hundred years. Our analysis will focus on his frescoes in the Arena Chapel at Padua. The intent will be to show that Giotto's stylistic innovations reflect a different religious feeling and purpose than does medieval Byzantine art. This difference can be expressed as an "incarnational" emphasis on the interaction of the sacred and the secular, as opposed to a dualistic juxtaposition of the divine and the mundane. The analysis of Michelangelo will focus on his Medici Chapel in the church of San Lorenzo in Florence. This chapel is chosen because it allows a demonstration of how orthodox Renaissance theology can appropriate and subordinate themes and images of the Ancient Wisdom revived by Ficino and the Platonic Academy. More specifically, this examination will develop parallels between Michelangelo's iconography and Ficino's concept of the soul and the relation of the micro- and macrocosm.

Giotto

Our primary interests here are in Giotto's views of man, God, and the world as presented in his masterpiece—the frescoes of the life of Christ in the Arena Chapel in Padua. To set the context for this analysis, however, it is helpful to compare his artistic style and religious views with those of his Sienese contemporary, Duccio. Such a comparison is frequently used by art historians to underscore Giotto's stylistic innovations. Our focus on the shift in style is intended to lead to a discussion of a shift in religious function. This comparison will be made by examining differences in their depictions of the Madonna and Child.

Duccio's *Rucellai Madonna and Child* (fig. 1) is done in the typical Byzantine iconic style.[1] The purpose of these icons is to facilitate devotion and worship by minimizing the mundane and emphasizing the spiritual. The Madonna and Child are therefore set against a gold background rather than placed in a natural setting. The gold background not only negates the ordinary surroundings, it is itself a symbol of beauty, immortality, and divinity. Similarly, the representation of human figures in iconic paintings minimizes the material or the corporeal. Duccio's figures, consequently, remain two-dimensional, almost like paper dolls pasted onto a flat surface.

Giotto's *Ognissanti Madonna and Child* (fig. 2) stands in sharp contrast to this iconic style. The throne, which appears to be made of marble, is set in a natural background. Moreover, the figures have weight and mass that produce a sense of corporeality. There is also a sense of linear perspective and an organized focal point that is absent from Duccio's painting.

One explanation of the marked differences in the work of Duccio and Giotto is that they reflect distinctions between the medieval religious outlook and that of the emerging secular Renaissance. This humanistic,

---

1. For a fuller comparison of the theological perspectives and religious functions of Duccio's and Giotto's paintings, see John W. Dixon, Jr., "Painting as Theological Thought: The Issues in Tuscan Theology," in *Humanities, Religion and the Arts Tomorrow*, ed. Howard Hunter (New York: Holt, Rinehart and Winston, 1972), 134-59.

Figure 1. Duccio, *Rucellai Madonna*, Uffizi, Florence.

Christian and Neoplatonic Themes in Renaissance Art 63

Figure 2. Giotto, *The Ognissanti Madonna*, Uffizi, Florence.

secular viewpoint is equated with Giotto's natural settings, organized perspective, and graceful, three-dimensional bodies. The position developed here, however, maintains that the contrast between Duccio and Giotto is not between traditional medieval religion and Renaissance humanism, but between two forms of Christian religious experience. Duccio represents a metaphysical dualism in which the sacred and the secular are ultimately incommensurable. Hence the secular has to be transcended to experience fully the divine. Giotto's is an incarnational view in which the sacred and the secular are intertwined. In this view worship and salvation do not depend on transcendence of the world. The religious task is instead to discover the divine presence in the world and to live a Christian life within it. Duccio's religious purpose is to transport the worshiper away from the world; Giotto's is to draw the observer into Christian participation into the world. The same emphasis on the intersection of the sacred and the secular permeates the frescoes of the Arena Chapel. In order to develop the principal incarnational themes, a brief description will be offered of the subject matter and artistic treatment of several of the panels. With this background established, it will be possible to examine the relation of Giotto's theology to his stylistic innovations.

Thematic Analysis of the Arena Chapel

In 1300 Enrico Scrovegni purchased property in Padua that included the site of a Roman amphitheater, where he built a family palace and a chapel dedicated to Santa Maria Annunziata. The chapel was consecrated on the Feast of the Annunciation, March 25, 1305. Bernardino Scardeone's history of Padua, written in 1336, indicates that the motive for building the chapel was to help expiate the sins of usury that hung over the Scrovegni family since the time of Enrico's father, Reginaldo, who was a notorious usurer.[2] In fact, building the chapel seems to have been a necessary condition for Enrico to be able to inherit from Reginaldo, since a usurer's property was usually confiscated.[3] There are no records of the commission or contract between Giotto and Enrico. There is sufficient cir-

---

2. Bernardino Scardeone, *De Antiquitate urbis Patavii et claris civibus Patavinis* (Basel, 1560), 332–33. Reginaldo's notoriety is reflected by the *Divine Comedy*, in which Dante relegates him to hell (*Inferno*, xvii, 43–78).
3. For brief accounts of the circumstances surrounding the Scrovegni and the building of the chapel, see James H. Stubblebine, ed., *Giotto: The Arena Chapel Frescoes* (New York: Norton, 1969), and Eugenio Battisti, *Giotto: A Biographical and Critical Study*, vol. 32 of *The Taste of Our Time*, trans. James Emmons and ed. Albert Skira (Lausanne: Skira, 1960).

cumstantial evidence, nevertheless, to make it certain that Giotto did the frescoes and may have even been consulted before the chapel was built.

Giotto's frescoes tell the story of Joachim and Anna, Mary and Joseph, and Christ. The north and south walls are covered with three bands of paintings (fig. 3): the upper tier depicts scenes from the life of Joachim and Anna; the middle and lower tiers show the early life of Mary, her marriage to Joseph, and the birth, ministry, Crucifixion, and Resurrection of Christ. The Annunciation, which is a central theme for the chapel, is placed in a prominent position over the altar arch, and the Last Judgment is over the entry portal on the west wall. This fresco program has received considerable scholarly attention, and several studies detail the intricate arrangement, interconnections, and symbolic positioning of the panels. Such a comprehensive analysis is beyond the present purpose. What is needed here is an examination of several panels that will provide a basis for assessing Giotto's theological perspective on man and the world.

The first panel on the north wall begins the story of the Holy Family with the expulsion of Joachim from the temple (fig. 4). Joachim and his wife Anna are much like Abraham and Sarah of the Old Testament. They are a devout, God-fearing couple who have been denied the blessings of children. Childlessness in biblical and early modern times was not regarded as a biological problem; it was a spiritual problem due to some blemish or sin. However, Joachim and Anna (like Abraham and Sarah) had led devout lives and could not understand their childlessness. Nevertheless, they did not question God and did not lose their faith. The first panel shows that the reaction of religious leaders to their plight was not tolerant or forgiving. Fearing that Joachim's pollution would contaminate the community and stain the sacred ceremonies, the High Priest refused to allow him to offer a sacrifice during High Holy days. Giotto has used gestures and facial expression economically to portray both Joachim's anxiety and his righteous indignation. The next scene presents Joachim after he has retreated into the countryside and is surrounded by his shepherds, the flock, and the attentive little dog (fig. 5). Although the rugged terrain in this panel recalls the cold, polished surface of the temple, there is a warmth of emotion here that is missing from the first panel. Joachim's dejection is tempered by the compassion of the shepherds and by the fretful efforts of the little dog to comfort him.

In the next two frames (figs. 6 and 7), Joachim makes a sacrifice that is obviously pleasing to God. When he falls asleep, he is visited by an angel who tells him that God has saved him and Anna for a special role: to be the parents of the mother of God. Other panels show that a messenger visits Anna simultaneously and tells her the same good news. This leads

66   The Modern Age and the Recovery of Ancient Wisdom

Figure 3. Giotto, Interior of Arena Chapel looking toward altar, Padua.

Figure 4. Giotto, *Joachim's Expulsion from the Temple,* Arena Chapel, Padua.

to the reunion of Joachim and Anna outside the city gate (fig. 8). Here Giotto has communicated the human love and affection that bonds Joachim and Anna as they await the divine event. The next several panels depict the birth of Mary, her dedication at the temple, the contest to select her husband, and her marriage.

The Annunciation is compellingly rendered in frescoes over the archway of the altar wall (see fig. 3). The top portion is set in Heaven, while the lower area portrays the Archangel's appearance to Mary. In the heavenly section the angels and the saints look on anxiously as the scene below is about to unfold (fig. 9). They look anxiously toward these events because they have the prescience to know the consequences of what is about to occur. Through the lives of Joachim and Anna, Mary and Joseph, the divine will enter into human history and transform it

Figure 5. Giotto, *Joachim's Return to the Shepherds,* Arena Chapel, Padua.

forever. The forthcoming birth, Crucifixion, and Resurrection of the Savior are not events in ordinary time and history—they are the fulfillment of time and history. Giotto's treatment of Mary blends an ordinary emotion with awe (fig. 10). Mary has been in the act of devotion when the angel appears. The positioning of her hands is fairly conventional, but it is almost as if she is cradling the promised Child in her arms, and the subdued, anxious look on her face reflects the apprehension of a mother who knows that her son must suffer and die in order to fulfill his divine mission.

This fresco is followed by scenes of the journey to Bethlehem and the Nativity. The visit of the Magi (fig. 11) again combines heavenly portents—the star has attracted wise men from the far corners of the world—with the more mundane events of everyday life. An attendant is trying to keep a stubborn camel quiet while the Magi pay their respects. This motif of the divine coinciding with the humble conditions of human

Christian and Neoplatonic Themes in Renaissance Art

Figure 6. Giotto, *The Sacrifice of Joachim,* Arena Chapel, Padua.

Figure 7. Giotto, *The Dream of Joachim,* Arena Chapel, Padua.

Figure 8. Giotto, *The Meeting at the Golden Gate,* Arena Chapel, Padua.

Figure 9. Giotto, *Prologue in Heaven* (detail), Arena Chapel, Padua.

Figure 10. Giotto, *The Annunciation of the Virgin* (detail), Arena Chapel, Padua.

existence is repeated throughout many panels, and it is a theme to be analyzed more carefully further on.

The next several panels cover the flight from Egypt, Jesus teaching in the temple as a child, the baptism, and the proof of Jesus' divinity through the workings of miracles. The first miracle occurs at the wedding feast at Canaan (fig. 12), where Christ changes water into wine. The corpulent host, who obviously enjoys fine wine, stands in marked contrast to the aesthetic figure common in the Byzantine style and gives solid evidence that Giotto has a very different understanding of human nature

Figure 11. Giotto, *The Adoration of the Magi*, Arena Chapel, Padua.

Figure 12. Giotto, *The Wedding Feast at Cana*, Arena Chapel, Padua.

and of man's relation to God. The next miracle is the raising of Lazarus (fig. 13), and then there are several panels portraying the triumphal entry into Jerusalem, the cleansing of the Temple, the betrayal, the mock trial, and the Crucifixion. These are followed by the Lamentation (fig. 14), in which the Crucifixion of the Son of God is seen as a cosmic catastrophe. The angels writhe in agony while Jesus mother and friends are stricken with grief. Taken together, these two sets of figures present the commingling of the human and the divine, the sacred and the secular. The remaining panels depict Jesus reappearance outside his tomb, his reappearance to his disciples, and his ascension. The last fresco of the series is a rendering of the triumphant Christ over the entry door (fig. 15). This scene returns the events in the world back to the heavens where the story had begun. Giotto's Christ conveys a sense of expectation, as if the Last Judgment, the next decisive event in human and divine history, is near at hand.

This cursory examination of the themes and the style of the frescoes provides sufficient background to allow an analysis of Giotto's important stylistic innovations in the handling of perspective, corporeality, and gesture. Perspective and naturalism are both present in the Arena Chapel frescoes. The sacred story of the birth, death, and Resurrection of the Savior is placed within a natural setting. Not only is the setting more natural than that of the Byzantine icons, the panels are organized around a single perspective that gives a sense of three-dimensionality to the work and establishes a point of view for the observer. In fact, the panels appear to be stage settings for the biblical drama and are intended to create a sense of identification between the observer's own world and the religious scenes. Giotto's treatment of bodies is also quite different from that of the Byzantine icons. There is no effort to minimize the physical. Bodies have corporeality and occupy a natural space on Giotto's stage. What is more, much of the dramatic action in the panels is communicated through body language. The gestures and facial expressions move away from ritualized posturing into natural movements that the observer can immediately recognize and identify with.

Do the stylistic innovations signal a fundamentally different world feeling than the Byzantine iconic representations? Is this the beginning of the spirit of individualism, secularism, and humanism that comes to characterize the Renaissance as a whole? Of course, the way the questions are formulated suggests the answer. Giotto's worldview is fundamentally different from Duccio's, but it is not a difference between medieval religious feelings and Renaissance secular feelings. The difference in theological views can be described as the contrast between a dualistic, ascetic theology and an incarnational theology. There is no question that

Figure 13. Giotto, *The Resurrection of Lazarus,* Arena Chapel, Padua.

Figure 14. Giotto, *The Lamentation,* Arena Chapel, Padua.

Christian and Neoplatonic Themes in Renaissance Art 75

Figure 15. Giotto, *The Last Judgment,* Arena Chapel, Padua.

Giotto's treatment of the body, its gestures, and the psychological interaction of the figures all contribute to an affirmation of human dignity, morality, and individual worth. In many panels, the unfolding drama centers around the human capacities for love, courage, honor, and reverent obedience. In fact, it is these attributes that give life its meaning and establish parameters for human action and dignity. Although these are attributes that for the most part fit completely into the secular ideal of human dignity, they are equally consistent with Christian virtue. Moreover, when the full iconography is taken into account, the worldview is decidedly Christian and not secular and humanistic.

The Prologue in Heaven (fig. 9) and the enthroned Christ (fig. 15) are heavenly scenes that bracket what happens in the world. Moreover, several panels depict God's entry into the world to give human life its direction, meaning, and purpose. The natural world and the life of man are arenas within which the divine drama unfolds and history gains its meaning and direction. God is the source of this meaning and purpose, but man has an active role to play as well. In scene after scene, the action centers around the lives of ordinary human beings who have the moral and religious sensitivity to attune their lives to the important events occurring in the world. These figures stand in contrast to other human beings who lack the moral and religious sensitivity to recognize the extraordinary events taking place because they are preoccupied with the mundane. Through the repetition of this theme, it becomes clear that those who are most truly human are those who are sensitive to the unfolding spiritual drama. Those who fail to recognize the divine within the mundane have a diminished sense of humanity. The world feeling that is conveyed, then, is not one of secularism but of the incarnation: the meeting of the human and the divine, the physical and the spiritual, the temporal and the eternal. This interplay sets the stage for the full range of human experience, and it is in this context that mankind either attains the dignity and purpose of life that God intends or allows it to slip by.

This worldview remains a basic component of Renaissance art and religion for the next two centuries and is already evident in Michelangelo's work.

Christian and Neoplatonic Themes in the Medici Chapel

This analysis of the iconography of Michelangelo's Medici Chapel has two purposes: to demonstrate the persistence of Christian incarnational or immanentist themes in the High Renaissance and to establish the compatibility of this Christian view with Neoplatonic/Hermetic themes and images that come to prominence through Ficino and the Platonic Academy. The next chapter's analysis of Botticelli's paintings will then focus on elements of Hermetic immanentism and magic that move beyond the boundaries of orthodoxy.

The Medici Chapel justifies Vasari's claim that the three fields of art had reached their pinnacle in Michelangelo's mastery of architecture, sculpture, and painting. Michelangelo was brought into the planning and design of the chapel from the beginning. He had a direct influence on the external as well as the internal architecture, and it is evident that he intended to combine painting and sculpture to create a uniform artistic program. The program that emerges is a unification of Neoplatonic cosmological imagery with distinctively Christian salvation imagery. As a result, the chapel is to be understood as a Neoplatonic cosmion, a little world in which the interrelationship between the elements of the external world are related to the inner life of humankind. As we will see below, the final thrust of this symbolic program is not a Neoplatonism that is irreconcilable with Christianity, as the distinguished art historian Erwin Panofsky has claimed; instead, the work reflects Ficino's belief that the symbolizations of the *prisca theologia* carry the same truth as Christianity but in a different form and that the proper reading of these symbols is possible only after the Christian event gives them clarity. Before turning to the analysis of this chapter, however, it is important to at least briefly sketch a background for Ficino, Michelangelo, and the commission of the Medici Chapel. This material will provide support for an argument that Michelangelo was influenced by Neoplatonic ideas and that a Neoplatonic Christian program would be suitable for the Medici Chapel.

There are, of course, no direct ties between Ficino and Michelangelo. Ficino precedes Michelangelo by fifty years. The contact between the two, therefore, is found in the profound influence that Ficino's Platonic Academy had on literature, art, philosophy, and the culture or *mentalité* of the age. Contemporary documents and subsequent scholarship leave no doubt that Ficino's theory of Platonic love permeated the poetry and literature of the Renaissance in Italy and the rest of Europe and that it served as an interpretive framework for the reading of classical texts. Platonic love, which differentiates natural love and celestial love, was closely tied to the *psychomachia,* the struggle within the soul between the lower soul, which connected man to material existence, and the higher soul, which connected man's spiritual nature to God. Ficino's writings and those of his followers used a wide range of imagery and metaphor to develop this basic theme, and its presence in the work of Michelangelo is an uncontested fact in Renaissance iconography. Michelangelo's exposure to these themes occurred during his presence in the Medici court, which, as we have noted, supported the Platonic Academy at Carregi and included within its circle several members of the Academy, as well as writers like Landino, Poliziano, and even Lorenzo himself.

As we have seen in the earlier discussion of Ficino, his work included a cosmological linking of the microcosmic soul to the macrocosm's. This cosmological dimension is also a prominent part of the Medici worldview. Lorenzo and other members of the family paid close attention to the influence of the heavens on individual lives and on political events, and as Janet Cox-Rearick has shown, the Medici cast their destiny and the destiny of Florence in relation to astrological events.[4] The same planetary deities that governed the spring season are the planetary deities of Florence and were those accompanying the reemergence of Medicean control there. Cox-Rearick's interpretation focuses on the artist Pontormo, the Medici Pope Leo X, and the secular rulers, the two Cosimos. The evidence, however, is clear that on at least two occasions Michelangelo developed this same integration of the microcosm and the macrocosm into a unified depiction of the relationship of man, the world, and God—the tomb of Julius II and the Medici Chapel.

The Medici Chapel

The Medici Chapel was added to the Church of San Lorenzo in Florence, which was the site of the Tomb of Cosimo, the great patriarch of the Medici family. The new chapel was to house the younger generation of the great political leaders in the Medici family—Lorenzo and Giuliano. In the original commission, the chapel was also to house two lesser dukes as well. The intent of this program was obviously to memorialize the great members of the Medici family and link the generations that had made Florence the financial, political, and cultural center for Europe. Michelangelo was brought into the planning of the chapel from the outset. There is evidence that he collaborated on part of the exterior design, including the cupola. His drawings and correspondence make it clear that he had full responsibility for the design of the interior. Pope Leo X, a Medici, freed Michelangelo from other obligations, particularly the Tomb of Julius II, so that he could serve the Medici on this project. Details of the political maneuvering that went on between the Pope, the

---

4. Janet Cox-Rearick, *Dynasty and Destiny in Medici Art: Pontormo, Leo X, and the Two Cosimos* (Princeton: Princeton University Press, 1984).

family of Pope Julius II, and Michelangelo's other patrons—even the squabbling over the cutting of the stone from the quarry—are intriguing pieces of social and political history that reveal much about the ebb and flow of the Medici fortune and the influence of the Medici Pope. There are also extensive records of several revisions due to financial and time constraints and to logistical problems of room size and the stone available for quarrying. In the end, the chapel was never completely finished, but Michelangelo's drawings and writings convey a clear sense of the overall design that was to blend the architecture, sculpture, and painting into a coherent whole.

Charles de Tolnay has provided a careful comparison of the Medici Chapel with medieval and classical funeral art, demonstrating that Michelangelo's treatment is unique.

> . . . the Medici Chapel is not an ordinary building destined merely to contain tombs, but a unit, expressing a definite idea-content. It is an abbreviated image of the universe. From ancient times religious architecture had signified more than a simple shelter for divine service. We know, for example, that already the Egyptian temple expressed in abbreviated form the universe, and that church architecture of the Middle Ages represented the Heavenly Jerusalem. Michelangelo goes back to this old tradition, but fuses the ancient conception of Hades with the Christian Beyond. In this new realm the souls of the dead attain for the first time since antiquity the dignity of philosophic contemplation of the supreme truth. The burial chapel becomes thereby the sanctuary of the true life of the soul.[5]

Three elements of the plan for the room itself are used by Michelangelo to create this image of the world. First, Michelangelo's redesigning of the cupola and his reworking of the windows in the upper region of the wall result in a strong sense of vertical movement (fig. 16). This verticality is augmented by the moldings and other trimmings, which direct attention from normal eye level to the light that suffuses the room from above. But the sense of verticality is tempered by strong horizontal lines that arrest the line of vision as it moves upward. This combination of strong horizontal and vertical lines creates several zones within the architectural framework that become important in the analysis of the Neoplatonic/ Hermetic cosmological zones. For now, however, the point to note is that the effect of Michelangelo's spacing and reworking of the light creates a room left in shadow from floor level into the highest regions of the walls,

---

5. Charles de Tolnay, *The Medici Chapel,* vol. 3 of *Michelangelo,* 6 vols. (Princeton: Princeton University Press, 1970), 74–75.

80   The Modern Age and the Recovery of Ancient Wisdom

Figure 16. Michelangelo, Interior of Medici Chapel viewed from altar, Florence.

Christian and Neoplatonic Themes in Renaissance Art

whereas the cupola is resplendent with light. Even without the specific imagery of the sculptures and the paintings, this structuring of the space already suggests familiar Christian and Neoplatonic juxtapositions of darkness and light as symbols for an earthbound, animalic, subhuman existence on the one hand and the celestial, divinely inspired existence on the other.

Before examining the iconography of the two tombs and their interaction with architectural space, it will be useful to review the pertinent features of the relationship between microcosm and macrocosm in the Neoplatonic/Hermetic tradition. The Neoplatonic cosmos is hierarchical. The lowest level is made up of preexistent matter that is brought into union with divine, ideal forms to create the material world. At the uppermost part of the cosmos is the realm of God. Between upper and lower is the earthly realm, the realm of the seven heavens or planets, and the sphere of the fixed stars. In the Neoplatonic/Hermetic worldview, the divine creation and maintenance of celestial and terrestrial order is mediated through planetary deities. There are seven planetary spheres (because seven is the divine number and the heavens are the realm of the divine). For each planet, as the names clearly indicate, there is a resident god or goddess from classical mythology: Moon, Mercury, Venus, Sun, Mars, Jupiter, and Saturn. The earth is created from the interaction of matter and the formative influences of the planetary deities (who are given their assigned duties by God). The influence of the heavens affects every aspect of the natural world. They account for the four seasons, for the growth of crops, for sickness and health, and for the physical and psychological condition of mankind. Even artistic creativity, according to Vasari, was a gift provided by the celestial influences. Physicians looked for the answer to epidemics in the conjunction of the planets, Ficino explored the use of celestial influences in regulating personality and in building psychological unity among people (military music, for example, invoking the influence of Mars, the god of war).

The planetary influences are absorbed or localized in the four basic elements of the earth: earth, air, fire, and water, which in turn are composed of the four contraries—hot, cold, moist, and dry. Each of these physical properties corresponds to psychological dispositions in human personality: the choleric, melancholic, sanguine, and phlegmatic. The complex interrelation of celestial influence and its reception in the material world can lead to a view in which terrestrial existence, including man's life, is completely determined by celestial events. This is, of course, the conviction of astrology; and astrology is a fundamental concern in the Renaissance period. It can also lead to astral magic—a topic that will become important in the analysis of Ficino's influence on Botticelli's paintings, which are examined in the next chapter.

Earthly existence is also segmented and hierarchical. At the lowest level there are inanimate objects, such as stones, that lack souls. Next come plants, which have "vegetative" souls; animals, which have souls capable of receiving sensations (sensitive souls); and humans, who possess intellectual souls. Man's intellectual capacity makes him different from the rest of the natural order and links him to the spiritual realm. Through the intellect, humankind is able to perceive the order, beauty, and truth in the terrestrial and celestial order and comes to recognize that the source of beauty and order in the world is God.

If we now turn to the sculptural program and the paintings that Michelangelo intended to place in the Medici Chapel, we can see how he has chosen to represent this elaborate interplay between the macrocosm and the microcosmic soul. For this purpose we can look at the tombs of Lorenzo and Giuliano (figs. 17 and 18). The first zone extends from floor level to the cover of the tomb. The second zone is the space in which the figures of the four times of day are represented. The third zone contains the statues of the two Medici, and above their heads there is a zone containing the thrones of celestial deities. In the arches above that zone, Michelangelo intended to paint scenes of deliverance or resurrection. The final zone (not visible in figs. 17 and 18) is represented by the recessed dome, the cupola, which is at the opposite end of the room from the altar. Michelangelo developed clay prototypes of statues that were to be placed in zone one, and it is generally agreed that these figures at ground level were to represent the river gods of the underworld. This would be the Neoplatonic/Hermetic realm of unformed matter (*hyle* or *prima materia*), the preexistent matter that divine creativity shapes into the world of time and nature (represented in the second zone by the times of day). The third zone, corresponding to the Medici figures, is an intermediate station between the material world and the heavens. Symbolically, the Medici are no longer part of the world of time; their actions in the world and the right orientation of their lives in the world have raised them above earthly existence and brought them to the celestial realm. De Tolnay has pointed out that Michelangelo's arrangement of the figures, who are sitting and looking out onto their surroundings, is contrary to conventions of medieval art, which usually depicted memorialized figures in a recumbent, sleeping posture. This transformation, de Tolnay and others agree, is used to represent the eternal souls of the Medici and not their physical bodies. It is a representation consistent with the differentiation of the soul's two dimensions. An uninformed, uncultivated soul is dominated by the lower part, which links us to the deadly, earthbound

Christian and Neoplatonic Themes in Renaissance Art   83

Figure 17. Michelangelo, Tomb of Lorenzo de' Medici, Medici Chapel, Florence.

Figure 18. Michelangelo, Tomb of Giuliano de' Medici, Medici Chapel, Florence.

existence. Cultivation of the higher parts aligns us with the transcendent realm and guides us beyond the world. More will be said about this particular aspect later in the analysis. For now, the point is that this concept of the higher element of the soul in close proximity to the celestial powers that operate in the cosmos is reflected by placement within the architectural space. As already noted, immediately above the heads of the Medici were empty thrones that Panofsky reminds us are well-known ancient symbols for divine presence. In the zone above were to be scenes from the Old and New Testament. These Christian elements and their relation to the Neoplatonic program will be discussed in detail below. For now the purpose is simply to complete the sketch of the Neoplatonic/Hermetic hierarchy. Above it all rises the cupola, which represents the realm of truth and beauty that transcends the finite world and even the realm of the celestial deities.

Panofsky has examined in detail the integration of human psychology and the governing principles of the cosmology as they affect the iconography of the Medici Chapel. Not all scholars agree with every aspect of Panofsky's interpretation. Nevertheless, there is general consensus that the Neoplatonic integration of physical, psychological, and intellectual relationships are part of the chapel's iconography. Therefore, Panofsky's description can serve to illustrate this intriguing interrelationship.

> For a Renaissance thinker it was self-evident that the four forms of matter symbolized by the four rivers of Hades could only be the four elements, Acheron standing for air, Phlegethon for fire, Styx for earth, and Cocytus for water. On the other hand these same four elements were unanimously held to be coessential with the four humours which constitute the human body and determine human psychology. And these four humours were in turn associated, among other things, with the four seasons, and with the four times of day: air was associated with the sanguine temperament, with spring and with morning; fire with the choleric temperament, with summer and with midday; earth with the melancholy temperament, with autumn and with dusk; and water with the phlegmatic temperament, with winter and with night.

In his interpretation of these physical and psychological influences, Panofsky draws a pessimistic view of matter as a trap: "The four rivers of Hades stand for 'all those evils which spring from one single source, matter,' and which destroy the happiness of the soul."[6] He also implies that this is Michelangelo's understanding of the quality of life in the

---

6. Erwin Panofsky, *Studies in Iconology: Humanistic Themes in the Art of the Renaissance* (New York: Harper and Row, 1967), 206–7, 204.

world. This is, I think, a misreading and not consistent with the juxtaposition of the two aspects of the soul, the lower and the higher, that is found in Neoplatonic philosophy and literature of the period. The world of matter does have a debilitating effect on the spirit and the soul. But this debilitating effect is possible only if humankind fails to cultivate the higher realms of the soul. It is obvious from the placement of the two Medici figures that this Neoplatonic program is a celebration of humankind's capacity to live life at its full potential in this world. Lorenzo's and Giuliano's lives were proper preparation for life in the beyond. Panofsky himself stresses that these figures represent two aspects of life properly attuned to the divine order—the active and the contemplative. Other interpreters describe the two figures as representing the intellect and the will, the two traits of the soul that carry it to an encounter with God.

Thus far we have concentrated on developing the Neoplatonic/Hermetic themes and images in Michelangelo's architectural and sculptural programs. It was noted at the outset, however, that these Neoplatonic images provided a context for the key Christian symbolizations in the chapel. It is now apposite to turn to the iconography that gives the chapel its overall Christian tone. We should note that the interpretation that follows is not consistent with that of Panofsky. Panofsky argues that Michelangelo's work during this period represents the decline of traditional Christianity and the growing influence of Neoplatonism. For Panofsky, the Christian imagery is part of the conventional decorations, an obvious element within a Christian chapel where the mass for the dead is celebrated. But he argues that Michelangelo's own convictions have now become increasingly Neoplatonic. On the other hand, de Tolnay and John W. Dixon, Jr., offer persuasive arguments that the chapel is organized to make the Christian images the focal point and that these images create the necessary link between the horizontal and the vertical planes leading to the cupola, the culminating symbol of transcendence.[7]

As already noted, de Tolnay describes the Medici Chapel as a synthesis of the realm of Hades with the Christian beyond. This synthesis introduces significant innovation into Christian funeral art. But it does not transform the basic liturgical function of the chapel, and the introduction of Neoplatonic elements does not compromise or diminish the fundamental Christian imagery. Both de Tolnay and Dixon have emphasized that the key to understanding the organic relation of the various components of Michelangelo's architecture, sculpture, and painting is to give

---

7. De Tolnay, *The Medici Chapel*; Dixon, "The Medici Chapel as a Resurrection," unpublished manuscript.

86   The Modern Age and the Recovery of Ancient Wisdom

Figure 19. Michelangelo, The Medici Madonna and Child, Medici Chapel, Florence.

full weight to the fact that this is a burial chapel in which the requiem mass is celebrated. The human point of view here is not the same as in a congregational chapel. In the normal arrangement the point of view is that of the congregation as it looks toward the altar. In the requiem chapel, however, the only human participant is the priest, and his point of view is from behind the altar toward the opposite wall (fig. 16). On that opposite wall in the Medici Chapel is a statue of the Madonna and Child, which is situated between two sculptures of prophetic figures. De Tolnay has pointed out that this placement of the central icon deviates from the normal congregational arrangement, and it must be deliberate. When the line of vision from behind the altar is understood as the primary focus of the chapel, it becomes clear why the two Medici figures are turned as they are. They, too, have their gaze fixed on the Madonna and Child. Symbolically, all eyes are turned toward the back wall and to the Madonna and Child at its center.

Therefore, it also becomes important to understand the representation of the Madonna and Child (fig. 19). The sculpture contains an interplay of passive and active forces; the spiraling energy of the baby stands in contrast to the placid, calm posture of the mother. As the baby turns with its hands pointed upward, attention is directed to the cupola above. In this single dramatic spiraling Michelangelo has brought together the harmonization of the horizontal and vertical forces that de Tolnay pointed to as being built into the architecture itself. The movement away from the darkness in the lowest zone to the highest rays of light above is accomplished through the movement of the Christ child. Dixon has stressed the contrast of the energy of the Child to the stillness in the figures of the Medici, who wait with great expectation because their destiny is clearly dependent on what is occurring before them.[8] This organization makes it quite clear that the basic message of the chapel is that the means of gaining salvation, of moving out of a dead existence in the world to full spiritual existence, is accomplished through the Madonna (the Church) and the Child (the Savior).

Given the centrality of this image, Panofsky's strong emphasis on Neoplatonic thematics must be questioned. It does not appear that Michelangelo has grown weary of the usual Christian imagery and turned toward the vivid symbols of Neoplatonism as the most suitable way of representing his own understanding of the nature of existence. It seems instead that he has found in the Neoplatonic symbols a prefiguring of the basic tensions in the human soul and sees in Christian salvation the culmination of the search for spiritual awakening that is so much at the center of the Neoplatonic imagery. This thesis is supported by the paintings that were planned for the upper zones of the chapel. A painting of the Resurrection was to go in one of the lunettes above the tombs. In a sketch Michelangelo made, the resurrected, spiritual Christ is soaring away from the tomb that had held him. This theme appears similar to Michelangelo's studies of the contrast between the body and the spirit in the tomb of Julius II, which had a sculpture of the disciple Matthew that shows the human form bursting out of the marble attempting to encapsulate it. Another figure, that of Moses, is described by Panofsky and others as a representation of the spiritual man whose soul is aflame with the divine. In the other lunette of the Medici Chapel, there was also to be a rendering of the Old Testament scene of delivery from the serpent (Numbers 21:6–9). This scene suggests deliverance at the hands of God in a tradition that prefigures Christianity, just as Neoplatonism prefigures the full revelation of Christian truth. The image would fit with both the Neoplatonic and Christian warnings for man to avoid being misled and find the true sources of deliverance.

Dixon's and de Tolnay's emphasis on Christian imagery produces an

---

8. Dixon, "The Medici Chapel."

interpretation far more positive than that of Panofsky. Panofsky's study of the Neoplatonic themes centers upon the tensions between the material and the spiritual and upon the ongoing struggle of the spirit for its freedom. Within the context of the Medici Chapel, this struggle has to be balanced against the celebration of victory. Lorenzo and Giuliano represent human beings who have so ordered their souls that they are able to move out of an ignorant, earthbound existence into a spiritually enriching one. The lives of these two figures show that the accomplishment of the spiritual quest and the pursuit of a life of meaning and purpose within the world are consistent. The one is preparation for the other.

Observations and Conclusions

The purpose of this analysis of Giotto's Arena Chapel and Michelangelo's Medici Chapel is to relate religious developments in the Renaissance to Blumenberg's analysis of the theological and philosophical issues in the epochal shift from the medieval to the modern. In Blumenberg's interpretation, the major issue in the medieval period centers on the problem of theodicy. Christianity's vacillation between affirmation of an omnipotent and loving Creator on the one hand and a loving, redeeming God on the other is the result of the failure to integrate or to choose between two ancient "pagan traditions." The first is the tradition of the ancient cosmos, which preserves God's omnipotence by emphasizing the role of subordinate deities in the creation of the material world and by faulting matter for its inability to absorb the divine. In this view the material world is not inherently evil, but it is limited; it therefore has the capacity to deaden or divert the spiritual quest. This view of the macrocosm has as its counterpart a concept of the human soul as microcosm. The human challenge is to orient the soul to the divine, and the key to this orientation (salvation) is right knowledge. In this tradition knowledge does not, however, provide a means of escaping the tragedies of the human condition. The definition of maturity is that of knowledgeable acceptance of the inherent conflict in life. The Gnostic tradition, on the other hand, views the cosmos as a prison and matter as a trap or tomb. The only hope for the soul is to escape the snare of earthly existence. Knowledge in this tradition means salvation from the world—an alteration of the basic human condition. This view stands in contrast to the classical philosophical tradition, in which knowledge brings acceptance.

According to Blumenberg's analysis, medieval Christianity attempts to exonerate God from responsibility for the unhappiness in the world by making evil the result of an original sin that distorts and weakens man's ability to seek truth and to serve God. Scholasticism's effort to reconcile its theology with a philosophical system that joins God to man and nature produces so many logical and epistemological problems that Nominalism is forced to reject the realist tradition. This Nominalist effort to preserve God's majesty leaves man increasingly to his own devices in making sense of the world and in attempting to deal with impediments to his happiness there.

The Renaissance Christian tradition that we have briefly examined shows that important theological and philosophical developments occur during this time that run counter to Blumenberg's organizing theme. The Renaissance Christianity of Giotto and Michelangelo affirms the beauty of the natural world but also acknowledges that a life that is not properly spiritualized can be absorbed into an animalic existence devoid of meaning and purpose. Neither Giotto nor Michelangelo stress original sin as the primary problem; emphasis is placed on the individual and the choice between the life of the flesh and the life of the spirit. An emphasis on the language of willing or loving emerges in this period in the vocabulary of Ficino and others. The good life can only be attained by allowing reason or the mind to guide the quest for the proper object of this love.

The emphasis on the two aspects of the soul and the importance of individual choice, so characteristic of Renaissance culture, is an important dimension in the history of Western experience that seems to be completely overlooked by Blumenberg. Certainly it has a substantial bearing on the modern development of the concept of human dignity, which plays a fundamental role in Blumenberg's definition of modern man. The work of Michelangelo also demonstrates that theological and philosophical themes that take shape during the Renaissance are at least as important as the medieval controversies between the Scholastics and the Nominalists. Ficino's effort to recover ancient truth and to integrate it with Christianity produces an immanentist view of the world that profoundly affects the understanding of human nature, the natural order, and man's relation to God. Because it is immanentist, it is also realist and therefore stands in contrast to Nominalism. The divine is present in the world through the mediation of celestial powers that have a direct effect upon individual lives and events. From Ficino's writings and from the Neoplatonic themes in the Medici Chapel, it is clear that this interplay between material and spiritual forces affects everything from human psychology and intellectual ability to the seasons of nature and to the vitality and welfare of a great political family and its homeland. The Italian humanists of the Renaissance dismissed the overwrought theological and philosophical systems of the medieval schools as empty speculations that had lost a proper grounding in human experience and in the basic problems of human existence.

As we turn in the next chapter to Botticelli, we will find yet another important component in this Renaissance concept of human nature and the natural order. Many of the themes are similar to those found in Michelangelo's work, but we will see that the Neoplatonic/Hermetic themes in Botticelli's art are much more closely aligned to Ficino's interest in the influence of the planets and the possibility of using the magician's knowledge to enhance those benefits.

5. The Hermetic Paideia in Botticelli's Art

The iconographic analysis of Giotto's Arena Chapel and Michelangelo's Medici Chapel established parallels between a Christian emphasis on the intersection of the sacred and secular and immanentist links between the micro- and macrocosms found in the Ancient Wisdom revived by Ficino and the Platonic Academy. This chapter will continue the exploration of Neoplatonic/Hermetic concepts and images in Renaissance iconography, this time focusing on works by Sandro Botticelli (1444–1510). Botticelli is chosen for two reasons. The first is that he is one of the earliest and most influential artists to explore the themes of classical mythology in his paintings. The second is that he, like Michelangelo, was a member of the Medici court circles influenced by Ficino and the Neoplatonists. In examining Botticelli's work, our specific interest will be on the depiction of the struggle between the higher and lower parts of the soul, the importance of knowledge to the cultivation of the soul's highest faculties, and the use of magic as a means of enhancing the soul's spiritual development.

We will focus on three paintings: *Minerva and the Centaur, The Birth of Venus,* and the *Primavera*. All were commissioned for Lorenzo di Pierfrancesco dé Medici (*Lorentius minor* or Lorenzino), a teenaged cousin of his namesake, Lorenzo the Great. *Minerva and the Centaur* appears to have hung in his apartment in the family palace in Florence, and Vasari indicates that he saw the other two at Lorenzino's rural estate, the Villa di Castello. The interpretation presented here assumes a thematic relationship among the three works, especially the two at the Villa di Castello—*The Birth of Venus* and the *Primavera*. It also makes assumptions about the significance of the fact that the paintings were for Lorenzino, in whose moral education Ficino was deeply interested.

This analysis of the three paintings draws upon and seeks to augment the iconographic interpretations by Seznec, Wind, and Gombrich.[1] Al-

---

1. Jean Seznec, *The Survival of the Pagan Gods: The Mythological Tradition and Its Place in Renaissance Humanism and Art* (New York: Harper and Row, 1953); Edgar Wind, *Pagan Mysteries in the Renaissance: An Exploration of Philosophical and Mystical Sources of Iconography in Renaissance Art,* 3d. ed. (Oxford: Oxford Uni-

though there are some important disagreements among these scholars about the sources and meanings of the subject matter of the three paintings, they agree on four key points: (1) Botticelli's mythological paintings are closely tied to the Renaissance recovery of ancient literature and art; (2) Botticelli's paintings draw upon and modify elements of the ancient mythology in the same manner that Poliziano and other humanists did; (3) these paintings are intended to serve as moral allegories or as representations of ancient truths concerning human nature, the world, and God; and (4) Ficino is a major influence on the anthropological and cosmological views expressed in Botticelli's paintings.

This iconographic approach is not, of course, the only tradition of interpretation and is certainly not without its detractors. Roland Lightbown, whose revised and expanded study of Botticelli has recently appeared, attempts to simplify the subject matter and intent of two of the three paintings by arguing that *Minerva and the Centaur* and *The Birth of Venus* were commissioned to commemorate Lorenzino de' Medici's marriage and that their allegorical references are limited to the power of Venus as the inspiration for love and marriage.[2] Charles Dempsey also offers an alternate interpretation by arguing that the subject matter of the *Primavera* is taken from the description of an ancient rustic calendar—an appropriate subject matter for a painting to be placed in the rural villa of Lorenzino. Dempsey's position is well documented and well argued, and it poses challenges to the interpretation presented here that are more direct than those of Lightbown. A comparison of the two will therefore be offered in the course of the analysis.

Questions and debates about subject matter, symbolic meaning, and ancient and contemporary sources present themselves because there are no extant contracts between Botticelli and his patron, nor are there any written records that would verify a direct connection between Botticelli's paintings and the work of Poliziano, Ficino, or other humanists or Neoplatonic/Hermetic philosophers. What is available, at best, are indirect ties between the three principals, Botticelli, Lorenzino, and Ficino, and a good deal of circumstantial evidence regarding the influence of Ficino on Lorenzino and those around him. The major points of connection must be briefly described before turning to the paintings themselves.

The central figure is Lorenzino, who was patron to both Ficino and Botticelli. Ficino's letters indicate that the two were quite close, and

---

versity Press, 1980); E. H. Gombrich, *Symbolic Images: Studies in the Art of the Renaissance* (Oxford: Phaidon, 1978).

2. Ronald Lightbown, *Sandro Botticelli: Life and Work* (Berkeley: University of California Press, 1989).

Lorenzino is remembered in Ficino's will. There is also evidence in the correspondence that Ficino was concerned about the young Lorenzino's education and was a strong influence on the young man's tutors. A letter that will be examined later on, for example, instructs the tutors to have Lorenzino memorize one of Ficino's moral exhortations. One of these tutors was a member of the Vespucci family, who were neighbors of Botticelli, and the art historian Gombrich speculates that the commission for Botticelli may have been arranged through Vespucci. There is, however, no evidence of collaboration between Ficino and Botticelli. Botticelli did, nevertheless, belong to the intellectual circles formed by Cosimo, Lorenzo, and Lorenzino de' Medici and would therefore be familiar with and influenced by Ficino, the dominant force in that circle.[3]

The analysis below is presented in two parts. The first is a brief examination of the relation of the paintings' iconography to Ficino's cosmology and anthropology. The second part offers a more detailed analysis of the paintings in terms of the Hermetic concept of *paideia,* the education toward fully human existence, as well as an examination of Ficino's views of the role of astral magic as an aid to education.

Minerva and the Centaur

In each painting a divinity is present who functions as a source of revelation. Minerva, Venus, and Hermes (Mercury) are entering the world and the life of man to awaken his godlike capacities for knowledge and to transform man's sensate, earthbound life into a life of transcendent knowledge and fulfillment. The least complex presentation of this encounter between unredeemed man and the messianic figure is in the painting *Minerva and the Centaur* (fig. 20). Minerva is, of course, the Roman goddess of wisdom who is born out of the mind of Jove (Zeus). Mythically and psychologically she is the opposite of Bacchus (Dionysus), who was born from the loins—the physical generative power—of divinity. In Botticelli's painting she appears with a centaur. This appears to symbolize a confrontation of cerebral wisdom and bestial nature, a familiar theme in Western art since the early Classical period. Perhaps the most famous representation of the confrontation is the battle of the Lapiths and the centaurs on the friezes of the Parthenon, the fifth-century B.C. temple and shrine to Athena, the Greek goddess of wisdom. Botticelli, however, is not representing a confrontation between men governed by reason and those governed by passion. Here a goddess is

---

3. For general background, see Gombrich, *Symbolic Images,* 31–81.

94   The Modern Age and the Recovery of Ancient Wisdom

Figure 20. Botticelli,
Minerva and the Centaur,
Uffizi, Florence.

confronting the centaur. Moreover, the centaur is not the wild, uncontrollable beast of conventional depiction; he is subdued, even melancholy. The bow and arrow beside him suggest that he is Chiron, who is mentioned in the *Aeneid* and was a popular allegorical figure in the Renaissance. According to the Renaissance tradition, an encounter with Aeneas awakens Chiron's consciousness that he is really neither a beast nor a human. He is a misfit, who is bound to his animalic nature and can only have the remotest glimmerings of what it must be like to be fully human. This tradition would account for his melancholy; Chiron is conscious of the grace and dignity of man and knows that he is unable to attain it.

Viewed from the perspective of Ficino and the Neoplatonic/Hermetic tradition, the centaur would be an appropriate representation of the soul of unregenerate, ignorant man—humankind without the aid of divine revelation. Although Ficino does not use the centaur image explicitly, it is consistent with his description of the soul in the *Theologia Platonica* and *De vita triplici*. In these works the human soul is the site and sensorium of all experience. The nether parts link human beings with the world of the body and the senses; the higher region joins divine and human reason. Moreover, there are passages in Ficino's other writings that urge his fellow man to awaken from the blind stupor of animalic passion and revive the highest powers of the soul, thereby opening humankind to the highest form of wisdom and truth.

> Wisdom, sprung from the crown of the head of Jove, creator of all, warns her philosophical lovers that if they truly desire ever to gain possession of their beloved, they should always seek the highest summits of things rather than the lowest places; for Pallas, the divine offspring sent down from the high heavens, herself frequents the high citadels which she has established. She shows, furthermore, that we cannot reach the highest summits of things unless, first, taking less account of the inferior parts of the soul, we ascend to the highest part, the mind. She promises, finally, that if we have concentrated our powers in this most fruitful part of the soul, then without doubt by means of this highest part itself, that is, by means of mind, we shall ourselves have the power of creating mind; mind which, I say, is the companion of Minerva herself and the foster-child of highest Jove.[4]

The Birth of Venus

Botticelli's *The Birth of Venus* (fig. 21) is based on the myth of the castration of Uranos, the god of the heavens, by Chronos, the god of time. When Uranos is castrated, his genitals fall into the unformed material resting below the heavenly vault. According to the myth, the mingling of divine potency and matter causes the spontaneous generation of Venus and the natural world. In his painting Botticelli takes up the scene just after the creation, or incarnation, when Venus is being carried to shore by the Zephyr winds. Botticelli's presentation of the episode in which divinity becomes incarnate in matter, particularly the treatment of Venus, fits Ficino's unique concept of the relation of man's love for terrestrial and celestial beauty. In his commentary on Plato's *Symposium,* Ficino explains that man's desire for eternal beauty is first awakened by the beauty of the natural world.[5] In order for humankind to find the

---

4. Ficino, "Five Questions Concerning the Mind," *Epistolae,* 705–12. English translation from Ernst Cassirer, P. O. Kristeller, and J. H. Randall, Jr., eds., *The Renaissance Philosophy of Man* (Chicago: University of Chicago Press, 1948), 193–94.

5. Ficino is the originator of the concept of the dual Venus. See his *Commentarium in Convivium Platonis* in *Opera Omnia,* vol. 2. For an English translation, see *Marsilio Ficino's Commentary on Plato's Symposium,* trans. Sears Reynolds Jayne, vol. 19, no. 1, *The University of Missouri Studies* (Columbia: University of Missouri Press, 1944).

96 The Modern Age and the Recovery of Ancient Wisdom

Figure 21. Botticelli, *The Birth of Venus*, Uffizi, Florence.

ultimate object of its erotic yearning, however, it must recognize that the natural world is but a limited manifestation or emanation of God through the limited and imperfect medium of matter and must transfer love of the natural to pure, spiritual science.

Ficino's doctrine of love seems to be strikingly presented in this painting of Botticelli. Botticelli's Venus is the incarnation of divine power in material form. When she appears to man, she awakens in him the love of divine beauty and truth. This twofold nature and function of Venus is presented in the following way. The unadorned Venus is about to be clothed in a beautiful wrap as she approaches the shore. The garment, given its floral patterns, is the gown of nature. Symbolically, the divine Venus is first found in the beauty of nature, but this is only a covering that must be unveiled, discovering the true celestial Beauty and Truth.

The *Primavera*

This dual figure, at once the natural Venus and the divine or heavenly Venus, is also central in the *Primavera* (fig. 22). Her two functions are presented through the scenes on her left and right. To her left, there is again the Zephyr rushing in from the heavens in pursuit of the maiden,

The Hermetic Paideia *in Botticelli's Art* 97

Figure 22. Botticelli, *La Primavera,* Uffizi, Florence.

who is once more an earth goddess. The results of this amorous activity is the beautiful young woman who occupies the foreground. To the right of the Venus figure is a trio of female figures representing the Three Graces or the three aspects of the soul in its pursuit of spiritual love.[6] The central figure, embodying desire, is turned toward the male figure on the viewer's far left, whose garments make it clear that he is Mercury. For the present purposes it is not necessary to present an extended analysis of the complex allegorical relationships among the figures. At present only the stylistic interrelationships that generate the overall movement in the painting will be examined. There is the movement initiated by the Zephyr emerging from above and descending in pursuit of the earth figure. The result of this movement is the beauty of the natural world, which is personified in Flora. This movement carries over into the other figures in the foreground. The Three Graces, representing the human soul in pursuit of beauty and truth, carry the viewer toward the figure of Mercury, who in turn leads up to the heavens. The combined movement, then, is an arc moving from the upper right corner back to the upper left. There is also movement from Venus, the central figure, up to the Cupid, who is

6. The prevalence of the Three Graces is discussed in Wind, *Pagan Mysteries,* 113–27.

shooting a flaming arrow toward the grouping of Graces on the left. It is worth noting that Cupid's flaming arrow (passion) is directed at the soul and symbolizes intellectual—rather than physical—love.

It is most significant that this painting has two revelational deities: Venus, the incarnation of divine beauty and the agent of divine love, and Mercury, the messenger who descends from the heavens to communicate the will of the gods to men, who are so easily lost when left to their own devices. It is also significant that Mercury is separating the mist that hovers over the upper part of the painting. It is through the agency of Mercury that the limits of human vision are overcome and the mist obscuring human perception is penetrated.

This brief description of the three paintings establishes general thematic links with Ficino's Neoplatonic/Hermetic views and sets the context for a more detailed analysis of connections with the Hermetic *paideia* and the role of astral talismans. The discussion of the Hermetic *paideia* draws upon Garth Fowden's *The Egyptian Hermes,* in which he describes the stages of an initiate's education into Hermetic truth as it is found in the *Hermetic Corpus*.[7] This *paideia* is based on the relationship of the master to the pupil (Pimander to Hermes) or of the spiritual father to the spiritual son (Hermes Trismegistus to Toth). The program described by Fowden corresponds closely to Ficino's relationship with the young Lorenzino.

The demonstration of links between the Hermetic *paideia* and the imagery of the *Primavera* will draw upon another, somewhat unlikely source, Charles Dempsey's "'Mercurius Ver': The Source of Botticelli's 'Primavera.'" This essay introduces important sources that link the subject matter of the *Primavera* to the basic scheme of the rustic Roman calendar detailing seasonal change in the farmer's year.[8] Dempsey indicates that his interpretation is offered as a counterposition to the claim of Panofsky and others that Mercury's role cannot be accounted for without a Neoplatonic exegesis or a metaliteral interpretation. I contend, however, that Dempsey actually helps to make the case for a metaliteral reading of the imagery, particularly in relation to the idea of the Hermetic *paideia*. I also contend that Dempsey's analysis adds further support for viewing the imagery of Venus and Mercury as planetary deities and therefore as part of Ficino's interest in astral magic and the use of

---

7. Garth Fowden, *The Egyptian Hermes: A Historical Approach to the Late Pagan Mind* (Cambridge: Cambridge University Press, 1986).

8. Charles Dempsey, "'Mercurius Ver': The Sources of Botticelli's 'Primavera,'" *Journal of the Warburg and Courtauld Institutes* 31 (1968): 251–73. Subsequent quotations are cited with page numbers in the text.

talismans. To begin my analysis, let me briefly summarize Fowden's concept of Hermetic *paideia* and then develop the pertinent parts of Dempsey's important essay.

The Hermetic *Paideia*

The purpose of Fowden's book *The Egyptian Hermes* is to situate ancient Hermeticism in its cultural milieu and to describe its distinctive religious and philosophical features. In a section entitled "Religio Mentis," he describes the philosophical *paideia* found in the Hermetic writings.[9] *Paideia* is, of course, the Greek term for education or instruction that draws out or cultivates the highest and fullest human potential. The Hermetic *paideia*, however, is quite different from the *paideia* described by Werner Jaeger in his famous three-volume study of the classical philosophical *paideia*.[10] The *paideia* described by Jaeger is the program of training that allows a young person to function as a free man in a democratic society. This education for citizenship ties together right knowledge with right conduct and equates personal virtue with civic virtue. A principal element in this education is recognizing the boundaries of human nature and learning to guard against the transgression of these boundaries.

The Hermetic *paideia*, by contrast, does not aim at acceptance of the world's existing conditions or acceptance of prevailing concepts of human nature. The program of education is aimed at making the initiate aware of the general state of alienation from humankind's true nature and preparing the way for a recovery of that nature. When it is recovered, the wise man is not content to accept prevailing conditions, but comes to realize that knowledge provides the power to control nature and perfect society. This concept of salvational knowledge, as already shown, is significantly different from the Gnostic concept that plays such a fundamental role in Blumenberg's work. In the Gnostic construction, salvational knowledge permits an escape from the world because it allows man to realize that it is a prison and not the proper home for man. This concept of *gnosis* is contrasted to curiosity (*curiositas*) about the world, which is a fascination that keeps man bound to his alienated condition. Hermetic salvational knowledge, on the other hand, begins with perception of the world's beauty and recognition of the divine forces that oper-

---

9. Fowden, *The Egyptian Hermes*, 95–115.
10. Werner Jaeger, *Paideia: The Ideals of Greek Culture*, 3 vols. (Oxford: Oxford University Press, 1939).

ate in the world. But the next crucial step, the ultimate step, is to transcend the realm of the world and the planetary influences to directly encounter the Creator-God.

Fowden points out that a crucial part of the Hermetic *paideia* is the emphasis on the relationship of the wiseman and the initiate. In the *Corpus Hermeticum* the one seeking knowledge is informed by the wise revealer of truth. Hermes, for example, is taught the truth by the divine messenger, Pimander; Hermes, in turn, teaches what he has learned to his son. Without the proper guidance of a master, there is a great danger of not only failing to obtain a proper education but of actually becoming disoriented and falling into a state of deeper ignorance and alienation.

According to Fowden's analysis, there are three steps in this education, each aligned with its respective topic: the nature of man, the nature of nature, and the nature of God. The first stage is to come to know and understand human nature, particularly to gain control of animalic instinct and emotion in order to cultivate the mind (*nous*). The second subject is nature, and the task is to see the natural world in proper perspective by studying the order and beauty of nature. Through such study the mind is cultivated and comes to realize that there is beauty in nature because God is immanent in it. The purpose of studying nature, however, is ultimately to transcend it by fixing the mind on God himself. The Hermetic *paideia* makes it clear that to stop at loving nature or merely being curious about it is to cut short the process of education. Remaining at this level does not provide salvation but leads to a blasphemous care for the natural order itself or to devotion to the subordinate deities regulating it. The step to the third level, that is to contemplation of God, requires a different form of intellectual activity. The rational analysis of sensory data about the order and beauty of the world must be set aside so that there can be a direct apprehension or attunement to God that establishes a like-mindedness (*homonoia*) with him. That is, human *nous* merges with or participates in the divine *Nous*. Put another way, man becomes God. It is through this attunement and participation that man acquires his godlike knowledge and his godlike capacity to control nature and perfect society, and it is only through this third stage that rebirth or restoration (salvation) is attained.

Fowden's description of the Hermetic *paideia* refers specifically to ancient texts, but passages in Ficino's writings make it clear that they contain the same features. This general similarity, however, still does not establish a connection with the paintings or their patron. To make this link, it is necessary to recall that Lorenzino was a young man, and Ficino was regarded as his master teacher.[11] There exists between Ficino and Lorenzino, then, the master-pupil or spiritual-father-and-spiritual-son relationship comparable to that described by Fowden. Moreover, the three paintings seem to take as their themes the three components of the Hermetic *paideia:* the right view of human nature, the right view of nature, and the right orientation of the soul that carries its quest beyond the created order to the divine ground of being.

Minerva and the Centaur, as we have seen, represents the animalic and intellectual dimensions of the soul and contrasts existence at the subhuman level to fully human existence. Although Ficino does not make a specific reference to the centaur, a basic theme in his work is the transcendence of the animalic state of existence, and the description already quoted gives an example of his use of comparable imagery. It is important to note that this first step in the process is initiated through divine guidance or divine inspiration in the form of Minerva. Minerva, of course, is the mythological representation of rationality that transcends or escapes the bonds of the sensual or the physical (she is born from the head of Jove, as contrasted to Dionysus or Bacchus, who is born out of his thigh). The *Birth of Venus* fits the second stage in its emphasis on seeing within the natural order the source of that beauty and truth in the creative action of divine forces. The figure of Venus serves not only as an incarnational figure linking the spiritual and the physical, but also as the goddess of love inspiring man to move beyond the physical to love of the divine principles of order. In the *Primavera,* the next stage—the move to contemplation of the divine—is represented by the left side of the painting. As we have already noted, the Three Graces represent the soul, and in this depiction the soul has turned away from the physical and is being inspired by Cupid with a divine love of Mercury. Mercury, like Pimander in the *Corpus Hermeticum,* is a messenger sent by God to clear the way for the direct and immediate understanding of God and his intentions. Mercury is not an incarnational deity like Venus, but is closer to the concept of a rational or revelatory deity like Minerva. Assuming that there is an interrelationship between these paintings, the use of the Three Graces to symbolize the soul shows dramatically the transformation or redemption of the soul when compared to the depiction of the soul in the form of the centaur. The Three Graces do not have the repulsive animalic

---

11. For that matter, Ficino's correspondence shows that he assumed the role of master-mentor to Pico and most other members of his circle. See *The Letters of Marsilio Ficino,* 3 vols., trans. London School of Economic Science (New York: Ginko Press, 1975-1985).

character found in the centaur; instead, their beauty and dignity rival that of the deities present in the *Primavera*. This seems consistent with the third stage of the Hermetic *paideia*, in which true illumination occurs and salvational knowledge is obtained.[12]

Beyond these associations with the Hermetic *paideia*, I think it is possible to find within the paintings some indication of Ficino's conviction that the search for wisdom may be aided by drawing upon planetary influences. To establish the connection between the *Primavera* and the representation of planetary deities, I must now take a somewhat oblique path by introducing the argument developed by Charles Dempsey in "'Mercurius Ver': The Sources of Botticelli's 'Primavera.'" This is an indirect route not only because it interrupts the direct analysis of Ficino's relation to the painting, but also because, as explained above, Dempsey states explicitly that a primary intent of his essay is to demonstrate that there is sufficient ancient and contemporary literary evidence to account for the subject matter of the painting without having to invoke the metaliteral interpretation of Panofsky and others. My reading of Dempsey's evidence, however, does not find it necessary to juxtapose one interpretation to the other, but permits them to be seen as complementary. Let me first briefly sketch Dempsey's argument, then demonstrate how his treatment ties the subject matter to planetary deities, and finally, suggest an interpretation of a spiritual maturation or metamorphosis that is complementary to the physical maturation or metamorphosis he describes.

Dempsey uses sources from the fifteenth through the seventeenth centuries to show that Mercury and Venus are commonly linked with the coming of spring. A key text is a little book by Girolamo Aleandro, Jr., that offers an explanation for a syncretistic solar relief in the collection of Asdrubale Mattei. This relief depicts the sun as governor of the four seasons, which are represented by the symbols of Apollo, Hercules, Bacchus, and Mercury. In the pertinent chapter dealing with Mercury and spring Aleandro has assembled the classical texts that show Mercury to be a god of spring and the month of May and define his relationship to the other deities of springtime: Venus, Flora, Chloris, and Zephyr (Favonius). Aleandro quotes several ancient sources that associated Mercury, as wind god, to Zephyr. Spring begins with the advent of Zephyr, the west wind, and ends with the same "cloud dispelling wind" (Mer-

---

12. This would also fit nicely if one of the sources for this subject matter is the *Golden Ass* of Apuleius and the conversion of the donkey to its full humanity through the action of Isis, a revealer of saving knowledge. The possible connection is developed later in this chapter.

cury). Dempsey quotes a passage in which Aleandro connects Mercury with Venus, whose month is April, by recalling Mercury's union with Venus, from which Cupid is born.

> "Now who is there to deny us?" asked Aleandro. "We have shown that Mercury is the same as Favonius [Zephyr], and we have seen that he joined with that same Venus who was thought to be the goddess of plants and flowers. In Greek the goddess of plants and flowers was called Chloris (because of the quality of greenness), and in Latin she was named Flora (after the flowers). The month of April was given as much to Flora as to Venus, and the month of May which follows was dedicated to Mercury, as Plutarch says in *Numa*." (253)

For Dempsey the drawing together of classical references to Mercury and Venus as the deities of spring provides the means of interpreting the *Primavera* without having to invoke metaliteral interpretations.

> Mercury's behaviour, his curious isolation from the rest of the figures, and his presence in a group of otherwise normal springtime deities, have been the stumbling block to successful understanding of the *Primavera's* imagery. Now Aleandro's chapter on *Mercurius Ver* gives us good reason to suppose that we need look no further than the season of spring itself to account for his presence and behaviour. The problem now becomes one of focusing the evidence gathered in a seventeenth-century text [that of Aleandro] on Mercury's nature in a manner which will shed light on the meaning of a late Quattrocento painting destined for the rural villa of a Medici prince. (255)

The solution to the problem hinges upon realizing that the Villa Castelli was a farm. The celebration of spring contained in the *Primavera* can, therefore, be shown to correspond closely to the basic scheme representing seasons and the planets governing the seasons in the rustic Roman calendar.

> The first Roman calendar, traditionally held to have been instituted by Romulus, was not organized according to the turning of the solar or lunar year, but followed the changing seasons of the farmer's year. It consisted of ten months. . . . The third month of the rustic calendar, May, was dedicated to Mercury, as we have already learned from Aleandro, who quoted an inscription from a rustic calendar dedicating the month to Mercury and to Flora, and recalled Plutarch's testimony of this in the life of Numa. The rustic calendar is unique in this respect. (255-56)

Dempsey then turns to Poliziano's *Rusticus* to show that a possible contemporary influence on Botticelli developed similar imagery in his poetry and drew upon ancient sources to do so. Dempsey then notes that

104 The Modern Age and the Recovery of Ancient Wisdom

Botticelli has not only followed a number of literary sources but has actually combined them and added his own emphasis. Two parts of Dempsey's discussion here are important and will be developed at length because they are tied not only to the mainlines of his argument, but also to the thesis offered here. According to Dempsey, Botticelli has adapted passages from Lucretius and Ovid in the creation of the right side of the painting, which extends from Venus at the center through Flora and Zephyr on the far right. The relevant passages from Ovid's *Fasti* are found in section 5, lines 195–222.

> "I was Chloris, who am now called Flora," the goddess announces at the beginning of the passage, and at the end explains the significance of her metamorphosis: "Before, the earth was of one colour." Botticelli has represented this by showing Chloris dressed in a plain, unadorned shift. But as she feels green Zephyr's breath on her back and looks over her shoulder flowers spring from her mouth and merge with the flowered pattern on Flora's dress. As Wind observed, these flowers, like the merging Chloris-Flora, are represented in a double aspect. They are real, as can be seen by the fact that the fingers of Chloris's left hand pass both in front of and behind the pattern on Flora's dress (and also by Flora's trailing veil, which shows the flowers on her dress reforming themselves into those on the ground), and they are also emblematic, the pattern on Flora's dress. From Chloris emerges Flora, an elegant pictorialization of the poetic metaphor of the bare earth becoming newly mantled with flowers at the first breath of spring. (260)

Dempsey argues that the alteration made by Botticelli transforms Lucretius's description of a parade of springtime deities and Ovid's account of Flora's metamorphosis into a representation of the growing process of spring. "In the same way that Chloris, nymph of the bare earth, is transformed into Flora by Zephyr's blowing, so Flora, who scatters the ground with the first flowers of spring, grows into Venus, the goddess of April and the full ripeness of the season" (260–61).

This interpretation tying the right side of the painting to literary sources makes an important contribution to understanding the work. Dempsey's treatment of the left side, however, is not nearly as detailed either in terms of its literary references or in its effort to link the left side to the theme of metamorphosis that plays such an important role on the right. Only three pages of his long essay deal directly with this part of the iconography. Here he demonstrates connections between Mercury's placement, his holding of the caduceus, and sources cited by Aleandro, showing through these associations that Mercury's role is balanced with that of the Zephyr. He then draws upon existing scholarship to show that the Graces have been understood as companions of Mercury, as well as of

Venus; he also indicates that through their association or even confusion with the Horae they are understood to be the guardians of the gates of heaven and that this has a symbolic attachment to Mercury's function as well. The interpretation allows Dempsey to summarize the iconographic treatment in this way: "The season moves to its close in May and Mercury, in whose steps the Graces follow, their dance sweetening spring's maturity. As the Hours of springtime, they too endow the season with its fruitfulness. And a touch of sadness too, for the round of their dance, like the round of the year, underscores the transience of spring. With clasped hands they follow Mercury into summer" (266).

As noted at the outset, Dempsey's principal purpose is to demonstrate that the sources he refers to provide sound literary evidence to explain the presence of Mercury in the painting of springtime. These literary sources would appear to eliminate the need for a speculative interpretation that invokes elements of an occult metaphysical tradition. Although he succeeds in this effort, one wonders if the painting must be viewed in polemical terms. Must the evidence for the use of the rustic calendar and the planetary constellation associated with it preclude the use of other ancient sources? Would a combination of sources and levels of iconographic interpretation help to explain the momentum that carries the painting to Mercury on the left side (Cupid's arrow, for example, being aimed at the Graces and not at the action on the right side of the panel)?

To develop this line of inquiry, I would like to return again to the discussion of the Hermetic *paideia*. That discussion related the three paintings to the three stages of enlightenment. The *Primavera* was associated with the soul's turning away from the physical and even the spiritual found within the physical and turning toward direct contemplation of the divine. Could this pattern of development or maturation be the complementary pattern to the physical one described by Dempsey? The right side metamorphosis that Dempsey describes is also consistent with the description by Gombrich and Wind, who identify the dual nature of Venus. In this interpretation, the natural Venus and her accompanying deities transform the primary matter of the world into the beauty of creation through the infusion of divine inspiration. Similarly, the divine Venus provides the starting point for the mind's or the soul's recognition of the spiritual within the physical. But, according to the Hermetic *paideia,* the next step in growth is to move beyond the beauty of nature that is created by the subordinate spirits to a direct encounter between the human *nous* and the divine *Nous*. So why is it not possible to see the left side of the painting as the complementary spiritual maturation that parallels the physical maturation on the right? While this effort at reconciliation is certainly not consistent with Dempsey's purpose, Dempsey's work actually strengthens one of the basic ties to Ficino and raises again an intriguing tie with Gombrich's interpretation.

Ficino's *De vita* contains a section describing planetary influences exerted through the representation of planetary images. It is, therefore, significant that Dempsey's interpretation relies upon treatments of the deities of the *Primavera* as planetary deities. Venus and Mercury carry out the function that the sun has ordained for them in their season. But the influence of the planets is not restricted to purely seasonal matters. We saw in the analysis of Michelangelo that the interrelation of physical and spiritual in the Neoplatonic system is considerable. Moreover, the same authors that Dempsey draws on as ancient authorities for the rustic calendar also devote considerable attention to the influence of the deities upon the lives of individuals and events in history. Therefore, Ficino's emphasis on planetary influences upon intellectual abilities and health would be completely consistent with the sources and traditions that Dempsey employs.

These general connections between Ficino, astral magic, and the *Primavera* become more intriguing in light of one of Ficino's letters to Lorenzino. This letter contains an astrological exhortation not to be content with the fate that the stars decree, but to go beyond fate and work toward the fulfillment of his potential. In this undertaking, the young Lorenzino will be aided by the gift of Ficino. This gift, according to the letter, is gained by knowledgeably drawing upon the resources of the planetary influences. Two aspects of this letter are extremely important in light of our previous discussion. First, Ficino offers Lorenzino a gift that will allow him to attain a destiny that exceeds what had been granted to him by fate. This gift is closely connected to the notion of Hermetic *paideia* already alluded to. Moreover, the emphasis on attaining gifts that were not provided by fate suggests passages in the *De vita* in which Ficino talked about using planetary influences to aid in the quest for knowledge. There is evidence that Ficino felt an urgency that Lorenzino understand, because he attached a cover note urging Lorenzino's tutors to have him commit its contents to memory. Given the importance that Ficino attached to it and its significance for this interpretation of the *Primavera* and the other two Botticelli paintings, it will be quoted at length.

> My immense love for you, excellent Lorenzo, has long prompted me to make you an immense present. For anyone who contemplates the heavens, nothing he sets eyes upon seems immense, but the heavens themselves. If, therefore, I make you a present of the heavens themselves what would be its price? But I would rather not talk of the price; for Love, born from the Graces, gives and accepts everything gratis; nor indeed can anything under heaven fairly balance against heaven itself.

The astrologers have it that he is the happiest man for whom Fate has so disposed the heavenly signs that Luna is in no bad aspect to Mars and Saturn, that furthermore she is in favourable aspect to Sol and Jupiter, Mercury and Venus. And just as the astrologers call happy the man for whom fate has thus arranged the heavenly bodies, so the theologians deem him happy who has disposed his own self in a similar way. You may well wonder whether this is not asking too much—it certainly is much, but nevertheless, my gifted Lorenzo, go forward to the task with good cheer, for he who made you is greater than the heavens, and you too will be greater than the heavens as soon as you resolve to face them. We must not look for these matters outside ourselves, for all the heavens are within us and the fiery vigour in us testifies to our heavenly origin. . . .

In fine, then, to speak briefly, if you thus dispose the heavenly signs and your gifts in this way, you will escape all the threats of fortune, and, under divine favour, will live happy and free from cares.[13]

E. H. Gombrich, who was the first to call attention to the importance of this letter's parallels with the *Primavera*, has also noted that there are differences in the two that prevent linking them with certainty. Nevertheless, Ficino frequently offered this sort of exhortation and often presented horoscopes for friends and admirers. It is, therefore, appropriate to consider that this painting may have had an allegorical or talismanic, as well as a more literal meaning.

Dempsey's essay makes an interesting connection with another aspect of Gombrich's interpretation. Dempsey draws upon Ovid to demonstrate that the theme on the right side of the painting may very well be the metamorphosis of primary matter into the glories of spring through divine inspiration. Gombrich had also attempted to relate the subject matter to the theme of metamorphosis, but his source was Apuleius and not Ovid.[14] *The Golden Ass,* of course, is the story of the adventures of a restless young man who roamed about looking for experiences to satisfy his curiosity. As a result of his excessive curiosity, he is transformed into a donkey. The cure for this bestial metamorphosis is to eat roses, the flowers of Venus. The opportunity to do so occurs during a pantomime in which the judgment of Paris is enacted. Gombrich has pointed to some intriguing parallels between this pantomime and the *Primavera*. Venus enters accompanied by cupids, the Three Graces, and Horae scattering flowers. The similarities are not clear and direct enough to make the connection incontestable. On the other hand, the pantomime fits as well

---

13. Ficino, *Opera Omnia,* 2:805; translation from Gombrich, *Symbolic Images,* 41–42.
14. Gombrich, *Symbolic Images,* 52–55.

as many of the other ancient references that have been linked to the *Primavera*. Moreover, there is another relevant episode. Through good fortune the ass is able to escape and flees out of the town down to the seashore. As he falls exhausted, he experiences a revelation, and the deity who emerges out of the sea identifies herself as Isis and explains that she is also known as Venus and as Athena (Minerva). With her appearance, Lucian is given back his human form and is instructed in the mysteries that provide him with the full knowledge he needs to gain his salvation, thereby avoiding the fate of being dehumanized or falling prey to excessive curiosity.

As already noted, certain ties between the *Golden Ass* and Botticelli's paintings cannot be established. Its theme, however, does complement the general Hermetic course of *paideia* found in the three paintings. *Minerva and the Centaur* shows the tensions between an animalic life and a fully human life, and the imagery of the centaur and of the ass are closely parallel. Furthermore, deliverance is made possible through Venus or Minerva. Direct ties to the *Golden Ass*, however, are not necessary to sustain the main lines of the present interpretation. The description of the Hermetic *paideia* in Fowden can be combined with the basic features of several major scholarly interpretations to demonstrate that the Neoplatonism of Ficino and his circle, which would include Botticelli and Lorenzino, contains a view of knowledge and of the natural world that is fundamental to our general discussion and in sharp contrast to Gnosticism on the one hand and to the Scholastic and Nominalist controversies on the other.

6. The Prisca Theologia and the Modern Age

Previous chapters have shown that the Renaissance revival of the *prisca theologia* introduces views of man, nature, and God that parallel those Blumenberg identifies as characteristically modern. These chapters have also demonstrated that the *prisca theologia* plays a fundamental role in both epochal transition phases. It is present in the religious and metaphysical ferment of the Hellenistic period and represents an important tradition of salvation through knowledge. By failing to give it proper consideration, Blumenberg omits a principal alternative to the bipolar tension he perceives between the Platonic myth of the cosmos and the Gnostic images of the world as a tomb or prison. Blumenberg's failure to take the *prisca theologia* into account as part of the intellectual ferment of the fifteenth and sixteenth centuries results in the omission of a fundamental effort to synthesize pagan revelation with the Christian truth. The "new understanding" of man, God, and nature offers a resolution of the opposition between classical metaphysics and ancient Gnosticism that Blumenberg claims set the philosophical and theological agenda for both the medieval and modern periods. This chapter and the next carry the analysis of the influence of the Ancient Wisdom tradition upon the formation of modern epochal consciousness into the sixteenth and seventeenth centuries. The intent is to show that major figures of the period were drawn to the myths and symbols of this tradition as a source for understanding the disorder of their own time and for determining possible means to overcome it.

Four representative figures have been selected for this analysis: Cornelius Agrippa (1486–1535), Giordano Bruno (1548–1600), Tommaso Campanella (1568–1639), and Francis Bacon (1561–1626). The work of the first three will be treated in this chapter, with the purpose of showing how the *prisca theologia* contributes to mounting criticisms of theological confusion and ecclesiastical disorder during the period, thereby influencing the growing epochal division that linked the disorder in Christendom with symbols of darkness and death. The relation of the Ancient Wisdom to Bacon's utopian programs will be examined in the next chapter. Focusing on Bacon will tie the discussion to one of the major figures Blumenberg concentrates on and will thereby make it possible to develop a direct comparison between Blumenberg's interpretation and this one. Furthermore, concentrating on Bacon will also make it possible to broaden the discussion to a general consideration of the nature of modern epochal consciousness and the difficulties that Blumenberg and other scholars have had in moving beyond the either/or choice between the Renaissance or the Scientific Revolution as the origin of modernity.

Cornelius Agrippa

The preceding examination of the *Theologia Platonica* and *De vita triplici* has shown that Ficino was drawn toward the new understanding of human nature offered by the Hermetic texts. His principal aim in both works was to provide an analysis of the relation of the microcosmic to the macrocosmic soul and to demonstrate that humankind has the capacity to transcend the limitations of fate and attain a divine condition. The source of this transformation is knowledge of the cosmos, which the philosopher or magus employs to draw down heavenly influences. In the *De vita* Ficino prescribes methods of magic that improve health, lengthen life, and enhance intellectual concentration. Though he refers to forms of magic that extend beyond self-divinization (for instance, Hermes rule over his city by magical means), he does not concern himself with broad-ranging religious or political reforms. Similarly, Pico (his pupil and author of the famous essay *On Human Dignity*) concentrates on the mythic elements of self-divinization rather than on the broader application of magic.

Late in the fifteenth century and throughout the sixteenth century, however, there is a growing sense of religious and political disorder and a yearning for relief from it. This broadened apocalyptic expectation can be seen in the work of Agrippa, who was regarded as one of the wisest men of his age. In an early work by Agrippa, *De triplici ratione cognoscendi Deum* (1516), he describes the widespread corruption and spiritual disorder in the Church as evidence that Christianity had lost its anchoring in the primary revelations of God. Agrippa identifies two principal sources for this state of alienation and confusion. His primary criticism is directed toward the Scholastic effort to make theology compatible with classical philosophy. For Agrippa this enterprise shows a failure to recognize the distinction between knowledge provided through direct revelation by God and informed opinions derived from man's sensory experience and deductive reasoning. Agrippa is also highly critical of the revival of the Latin humanist tradition, which also places undue emphasis on human reason and imagination.

In describing the three paths open to man, Agrippa places conventional approaches in juxtaposition to true understanding revealed in the ancient teachings. In its broadest application this is a contrast between the intellectual disorder caused by Adam's squandering of the highest forms of esoteric knowledge and the magus's use of that knowledge to become a terrestrial god. From this perspective, nature—the first of Agrippa's three paths to true knowledge—can only be understood properly if one follows the occult teachings of the Ancient Wisdom. On this point Agrippa's position is similar to Ficino's effort to develop a cosmology that links the physical and spiritual worlds and connects man's knowledge of the cosmos with the power to restore nature and to perfect the human condition. His perspective on the law, the second path, derives from the Cabalist tradition, which he is convinced provides the power to ascend through the orders of nature to direct communion with God.[1] Thus man gains full knowledge of the workings of nature and the operative power to change the conditions of existence. The return to the gospel, the third path, occurs through a reading of the *prisca theologia,* clarifying the role God wants man to assume.

This brief discussion indicates that Agrippa continues the efforts of Ficino and Pico to establish the unifying core of the revelations given by God and to use it to recover the full understanding of human nature. For Agrippa man's true condition is the one described in the Egyptian Genesis. God created man to be a terrestrial god. For reasons that are never clear, however, man becomes disoriented and alienated from his true nature. To guide man back, God has provided the *prisca theologia*. Again for unexplained reasons, man lost the ability to understand and use it. Now, however, recovering the hidden truth of the Ancient Wisdom allows Agrippa and other wise men to gain a comprehensive understanding of these revelations and thereby recognize the source of man's alienation and overcome it. It is with this conviction that Agrippa undertook his famous text, *De occulta philosophia.*

The *De occulta* was one of the most widely known texts in the sixteenth century, and it contributed to Agrippa's growing international reputation as the master magician of his age. In a later work, *Incertitudine et Scientarum et Artium,* Agrippa criticizes conventional philosophy and

---

1. Pico was a principal contributor to the development of a Christianized Cabala; see Frances Yates, *The Occult Philosophy in the Elizabethan Age* (London: Routledge and Kegan Paul, 1979), especially chapter 2. For a discussion of Agrippa's Cabala, see Yates, *Occult Philosophy,* chapters 5 and 6. For a general discussion of the development of the Christianized Cabala, see J. L. Blau, *The Christian Interpretation of the Cabala in the Renaissance* (Port Washington, N.Y.: Kennikat Press, 1944), and François Secret, *Les Kabbalistes chrétiens de la Renaissance* (Paris: Dunod, 1963).

theology, the revival of humanism, and the distortion and corruption of God's revelation in the Ancient Wisdom. Little needs to be said about Agrippa's criticisms of the first two categories, since his stance is consistent with that in the *De triplici ratione*. The criticisms of the occult wisdom, however, do need explanation, and a closer examination shows that they are directed at two specific types. The first encompasses astrology and other divinatory systems. In fact, Agrippa, like Ficino and Pico, rejects astrology because its basic premise is that man's fate is knowable because it is determined by the stars. Agrippa maintains that man can use astral magic to manipulate the stars and other celestial divinities to serve his own purpose and to alter his fate.

Agrippa also criticizes the occult wisdom on the basis of the Hermetic materials and the Cabala. At first glance he does seem to be making a significant departure on this score, but closer examination shows that this is not the case. In Agrippa's view, the Hermetic materials were important, but they were not the primary source of ancient learning. Therefore, when he claims in the *De vanitate* that these materials in themselves are not a sufficient guide to knowledge and that if used by themselves they lead to sin, he is not significantly altering his opinion. His attack on the Cabala also turns out to be consistent with his earlier position. He criticizes particularly those elements of the Jewish Cabala that develop after the coming of Christ and show a deliberate disregard for the higher truth revealed by the Messiah. He continues, however, to value those elements of the Cabala that point toward the fuller Christian revelation. This position is consistent with that taken in both the *De triplici ratione* and the *De occulta*. Throughout his life Agrippa was convinced that the key to this revelation was not in the literal words of the gospel but in their secret, esoteric meaning that could be brought to light by use of the Cabala and other Ancient Wisdom traditions.

It is also important to note that Agrippa's views of the source of knowledge and the concept of man are not altered in the *De vanitate*. Magic is not included in the sciences that he criticizes, but is regarded as the highest form of natural philosophy. This magic is essential to restoring man as a terrestrial god and overcoming the alienated state produced by Adam's sin. Further evidence that Agrippa's position remained basically unchanged in his later years is found in an important letter to which Charles Nauert has called attention. In this letter, written two years after the *De vanitate,* Agrippa acknowledges that there are "natural sciences, metaphysical arts, and occult devices . . . whereby one can licitly defend kingdoms, increase wealth, and cure sickness."[2] This description is con-

---

2. Charles G. Nauert, Jr., *Agrippa and the Crisis of Renaissance Thought* (Urbana: University of Illinois Press, 1965), 216.

sistent with Agrippa's earliest position, which lauded the recovery of knowledge that enabled man to transform the conditions of his existence and to perfect society.

A brief review of Agrippa's fundamental concerns show that they are comparable to those of religious reformers of the period. His attacks on the corruption of the Church and the ignorance and error of both Scholastic philosophy and humanism are similar to those of Luther, for example. Both see the solution to the present disorder in a return to a pure form of gospel Christianity. Their understanding of what constitutes this pristine course, however, is very different. For Luther, it is realigning the teachings and practices of the Church with primitive Christianity; for Agrippa, it is recovering the hidden wisdom of the gospel revelations. Luther and Agrippa also hold fundamentally different views of man's proper relation to God. Luther sees a gulf separating sinful man from his righteous God, and only divine action can bridge it. Although Agrippa agrees with Luther's description of the human condition after Adam's sin, he is convinced that this unnatural state can be overcome through a recovery of the ancient knowledge. When man makes the effort to reorient his soul and recover his true nature, he will be restored as a terrestrial god capable of finding his purpose and fulfillment through action in the world. The basic contrast between the two is most concisely expressed in their respective views of Adam's sin. For Luther, the sin is man's desire to gain knowledge to be like God. For Agrippa, it is man's choice of a sentient life in which he worships the creation rather than the Creator, thereby disregarding the higher forms of knowledge that can put him in direct communion with God and enable him to be an active participant in the creation.

Giordano Bruno

There is a longstanding view of Bruno as a martyr to the cause of modern science. This view, which Edward A. Gosselin traces to nineteenth-century historiography, can be summarized as follows:

> An itinerant renegade friar, Bruno defied contemporary ecclesiastical authorities and doctrines. In addition, he vehemently rejected the commonly held Ptolemaic belief that the earth lay at the center of the universe, and engaged in mystical speculation which centered about his pioneering support of the Copernican view. In connection with his Copernican beliefs, he held also that the universe contains an infinite number of worlds populated with intelligent beings. On account of these teachings, Bruno was tried for heresy by the Inquisition and burned at the stake in 1600. He thus

became the first martyr of modern science at the hands of the Church, and thereby a precursor of Galileo.[3]

Thanks primarily to the work of Frances Yates, it is now clear that Bruno's commitment to the defense of the Copernican system stemmed from a very different source than Galileo's.[4] For Bruno the Copernican system represented a recovery of the *prisca theologia*'s view of the universe and signaled the beginning of a general recovery of the ancient tradition that would produce a thoroughgoing religious and political reformation. Bruno's vision of the beginning of a new age and of the messianic role he was to play in ushering it in is presented in one of his early writings, *Cena de le ceneri* (*The Ash Wednesday Supper*) of 1584, which is his account of a dinner at which he defended the Copernican view against the "pedantry" of Oxford's philosophers and theologians. This dialogue may initially seem to be similar to Galileo's famous *Dialogue Concerning the Two Chief World Systems,* in which the Copernican theory is defended against philosophical and theological criticisms. Closer examination of Bruno's work makes it clear, however, that the intent of the two works is markedly different. Galileo's dialogue focuses on empirical and mathematical issues in the debate over the two astronomical systems and implicitly defends the Copernican view as a more accurate and adequate account of observable phenomena. Bruno, on the other hand, devotes little of his dialogue to physical or astronomical matters. Instead, he celebrates Copernicus's work as the beginning of the recovery of Ancient Wisdom that, when fully developed, will provide the means for a thorough recovery from rampant social, political, and religious disorder. Again, the reform that is possible is not limited to "scientific accuracy"; rather, the Copernican reorientation is the signal of a recovery of the microcosmic-macrocosmic reordering of reality. Copernicus represents, in Bruno's words, "the dawn which must precede the rising of the sun of

---

3. Edward A. Gosselin, Introduction to Giordano Bruno, *The Ash Wednesday Supper,* ed. and trans Edward A. Gosselin and Laurence S. Lerner (Hamden, Conn.: Archon Books, 1977), 11. Subsequent quotations are cited with page numbers in the text. Gosselin maintains that this "myth" originated in the nineteenth century: "Since the Church of the late nineteenth century was obscurantist, antiscientific, and anti-intellectual, and since the late nineteenth century saw science as the standard-bearer of progress and enlightenment, it was easy to reflect the current situation back three hundred years and to cast Bruno as a martyr for science, a proto-Galileo. Bruno's support of Copernicanism, the seventeenth-century persecution of Galileo, and the retention of both Copernicus' and Galileo's books on the Index of Prohibited Books: all these together made a plausible case for a neat lesson with a fitting moral" (22–23).

4. Yates, *Giordano Bruno,* especially 190–397.

the ancient and true philosophy, for so many centuries entombed in the dark caverns of blind, spiteful, arrogant and envious ignorance" (87).

Two points are important in this darkness/light symbolism. First, the full sunrise refers to a thorough epistemological shift from the ignorance and error of present learning to a recovery of ancient truth. As we shall see in subsequent passages, Bruno finds Christianity, particularly the doctrinal splits between Protestants and Catholics, to be at the heart of the rampant disorder and sees the Hermetic wisdom as the key to resolving the dogmatic concerns that caused the religious and political convulsions threatening to destroy the world. The second important point found in the root image is the role that Bruno understands to be his. Bruno's description of his achievement in relation to that of Copernicus suggests that he regarded Copernicus as a sort of John the Baptist who paved the way for Bruno's own messianic role as religious and political reformer. In several passages Bruno indicates that his recovery and promulgation of the *prisca theologia* can serve as the means for overcoming the present state of social and political disorder and for achieving personal contentment and religious certitude.

Because the myth of Bruno's martyrdom for science persists and because Blumenberg attaches considerable importance to Bruno's epistemology and cosmology as elements of the epochal transition to modern self-assertion, *The Ash Wednesday Supper* will be reexamined and its affinities with the *prisca theologia* more clearly demonstrated.[5] The work consists of five dialogues: the first sets the stage for the others by explaining Bruno's ideas in relation to Copernicus's; the second consists of a symbolic description of Bruno's ordeal to reach the banquet room; the third contains the opening rounds in the debate on Copernicanism and its metaphysical meaning; the fourth examines religious objections to Copernicanism and contains highly symbolic references to learned ignorance and social disorder among the intellectuals as well as the masses; the fifth continues Bruno's explanation of the infinity of the cosmos, the infinite number of solar systems, and the animate nature of the cosmos. Of the five, only two are devoted primarily to physical or astronomical problems, and one of these contains flawed accounts of Copernicus and erroneous astronomical and mathematical calculations. The other three use Copernican heliocentrism as the context for a metaphysical discussion aimed at demonstrating the importance of the *prisca theologia* in resolving religious and political conflict through right knowledge.

---

5. Part 4 of *The Legitimacy of the Modern Age* carries an extended discussion of Bruno as a protomodern thinker (see 457–82, 549–86).

The symbolic tone and metaphysical themes are apparent from the outset. The first dialogue is primarily a recounting of the debate by an eyewitness, who is responding to questions from others who were not there. Their initial questions have to do with Bruno's adversaries: Did they speak Latin well? Were they gentlemen? These queries, which seem relatively trivial, introduce several important themes that run through the dialogues: the nature of learning (the reference to Latin as the language of scholars), the relation of knowledge to proper human behavior (whether these were gentlemen), and the question of communication. In one fashion or another these themes are found at the beginning of each dialogue, and subsequent developments make it clear that traditional learning has not brought social, political, and religious stability. On the contrary, it has contributed to the brutishness of both the elite and the masses, and the presumption of knowledge has made scholars blind to the truth. This central theme is reinforced by the persona of the dialogues. Prudenzio, for example, is a pedant and polymath who knows and cherishes much of the humanistic ancient learning but remains a fool, preoccupied with trivialities of grammar and style, unable to recognize what is most important in ancient learning.

The main theme of the dialogue and the work as a whole, however, is set out in Teofilo's comparison of the accomplishments of Copernicus and Bruno (Teofilo, "loved of God," is a pseudonym for Bruno himself).[6] Of Copernicus, Teofilo says, "He was a man of deep, developed, diligent and mature genius; a man not second to any astronomer before him except in order of succession and time. . . . This estate he attained by freeing himself from a number of false presuppositions of the common and vulgar philosophy, which I will not go so far as to term blindness" (86). Copernicus succeeded in transcending vulgar opinion because he "took up again those despised and rusty fragments that he was able to get from the hands of antiquity, refurbished them, and assembled and fastened them together again" (86). Through his revival of Ancient Wisdom, Copernicus moved learning out of the darkness that engulfed it. But Copernicus's work is only the first rays of dawn—his understanding and appreciation of the *prisca theologia* is limited to mathematics. The full recovery of the light from the Ancient Wisdom did not occur until Bruno appeared. Teofilo compares Bruno's heroic accomplishment to Tiphys, who invented the first ship, and to Columbus, "another Tiphys who discovered a new world." Bruno is superior because he

---

6. Bruno playfully has Teofilo admit that "it is not appropriate for me to praise him [Bruno], since he is as close to me as I am to myself" (87).

has ventured into the extraterrestrial, divine realm and "found the way to ascend to the sky, compass the circumference of the stars, and leave at his back the convex surface of the firmament" (88). As a result of his exploration of celestial powers,

> The Nolan . . . has freed the human mind and the knowledge which were shut up in the strait prison of the turbulent air . . . . [The mind's] wings were clipped so that it could not soar and pierce the veil of the clouds to see what was actually there. It could not free itself from the chimeras of those who, coming forth with manifold imposture from the mire and pits of earth (as if they were Mercuries and Apollos descended from the skies), have filled the whole world with infinite folly, nonsense and vice, disguised as so much virtue, divinity, and discipline. By approving and confirming the misty darkness of the sophists and blockheads, they extinguished the light which made the minds of our ancient fathers divine and heroic. . . . Thus, by the light of his senses and reason, he opened those cloisters of truth which it is possible for us to open with the key of most diligent inquiry; he laid bare covered and veiled nature, gave eyes to the moles and light to the blind . . . he loosed the tongues of the dumb . . . [and] he strengthened the lame who could not make that progress of the spirit which base and dissoluble matter cannot make. (89–90; last brackets are translator's)

Teofilo tempers this praise with a caution, however. Those who live in darkness often fear the light, and there are even some ignoramuses "who, because of some credulous folly, stubbornly wish to remain in the darkness of what they have once learned badly" (93).

At this point Prudenzio, the pedant and antiquarian, objects to Bruno's newfangled ideas and urges respect for the wisdom of the ancients. Bruno/Teofilo uses this objection to set forth two crucial points regarding ancient truth. The first is made somewhat playfully, but is clearly meant to be taken seriously. Teofilo, responding to Prudenzio, claims that "from your principle can be inferred the contrary of what you think. I mean that we are older and have greater age than our predecessors" (93–94). He then describes the progress made in astronomy, from its rebirth with Eudoxus, who lived near the time of Alexander, to the extraordinary rebirth eighteen hundred years later by Copernicus. This description, coupled with his earlier praise of Copernicus, establishes that it is possible for advances in learning to occur in the modern age; it is also evident that such advances are both a recovery of ancient truth that has become obscured and a discovery of new insights based on ancient teachings. Although the references made here are to Copernicus and astronomy, his earlier remarks about Bruno's relation to Copernicus make it clear that Bruno is responsible for the recovery and *advance* of ancient truth in its full dimensions.

In this context Teofilo makes another essential point about ancient and modern learning. He begins by observing that the age in which a scholar lives does not guarantee him wisdom. Even in the period of Ancient Wisdom there were those who "lived like corpses," dead to the truth around them. Similarly, in the present age many who pretend to knowledge remain ignorant (see 94). As noted earlier, this theme of ignorance among the learned runs throughout the dialogues. Teofilo adds another critical point when Prudenzio defends the ancient masters. He replies that the ancient learning cherished by Prudenzio is not the most ancient or the most learned.

> If this vulgar opinion of yours is as true as it is old, certainly it was false when it was new! Before this philosophy which suits your brain arose, there existed the philosophy of the Chaldeans, of the Egyptians, of the magi, of the Orphists, of the Pythagoreans and of others who spring readily to mind [and] who better suit our head; from them first rebelled frivolous and empty logicians and mathematicians who were not so much enemies of Antiquity as strangers to the Truth. Let us put aside, then, the question of the old and the new, seeing that there is no new thing which cannot be old and there is no old thing which has not been new, as your Aristotle rightly noted. (94–95; translator's brackets)

Subsequently, he makes a direct comparison between those who come to know the most ancient truth (Hermeticism) and those following the ancient learning (Aristotelianism) that fascinated so many of his age.

> The former are moderate in life, expert in medicine, judicious in contemplation, unique in divination, miraculous in magic, wary of superstition, law-abiding, irreproachable in morality, godlike in theology, and heroic in every way. All this is shown by the length of their lives, their healthier bodies, their most lofty inventions, the fulfillment of their prophecies, the substances transformed by their works, the peaceful deportment of their people, their inviolable sacraments, the great justice of their actions, the familiarity of good and protecting spirits, and the vestiges, which still remain, of their amazing prowess. I leave to the judgment of anyone of good sense the consideration of the fruits of the latter. (96)

In later passages Teofilo provides extended descriptions of the corruption and disorder that pervade society, and he repeatedly underscores the detrimental effects of present learning that are reminiscent of Agrippa: "Those who study under them will, in the end, have gained nothing more than to have advanced themselves from ignorance, which is a privation of truth, to thinking and believing that they know, which is madness and a kind of falsity" (98).

Into this state of disorder Bruno introduces his truth through the Socratic process of questioning and debate. The remaining dialogues show "how mighty his philosophy is in taking care of and defending itself, [as well as] in baring the emptiness and revealing the fallacies of sophists and the blindness of the common and vulgar philosophy" (100; translator's brackets). The blindness of common religion and vulgar philosophy, with their resultant disorder in society, is the second theme running through the dialogues. It is found, for instance, in the second dialogue's description of the filth, vulgarity, and bestiality of the London streets as Bruno and his companions make their way to the supper meeting. Having arrived and joined a small, genteel company, they can still observe the hoi polloi's vulgar celebration of the Eucharist. Although Bruno indicates that his noble companions do not follow the vulgar Protestant practice of "the passing of the cup," he is nevertheless aware that in most of England this vulgar attempt at communion between God and man and between man and man is underway on Ash Wednesday. Usually the goblet is passed from hand to hand all around the table.

> After the leader . . . has detached his lips, leaving a layer of grease which could easily be used as glue, another drinks and leaves you a crumb of bread, another drinks and leaves a bit of meat on the rim. . . . The meaning of all this is that, since all of them come together to make themselves into a flesh-eating wolf to eat as with one body the lamb . . . they come to form themselves into . . . one community, one brotherhood, one plague, one heart, one stomach, one gullet and one mouth. (127)

The remaining dialogues juxtapose this ritual to the spiritual communion possible through a recovery of knowledge. The ancient truth, as we have seen, extends beyond issues in Copernican astronomy to a complete description of the spiritual links between the microcosm and macrocosm.

The third dialogue centers around a debate between Bruno and Nundinio concerning whether the Copernican system is intended only as a computational device. Bruno disparages this interpretation as more of the vulgar foolishness of the time and invokes ancient authority for the truth of Copernicus's view. From here he moves increasingly from purely physical to metaphysical considerations. The fourth dialogue repeats the major themes of the first three. When the question of the conflict between heliocentrism and the Scriptures is raised, Bruno argues that the Scriptures deal with moral law for the masses, not with natural philosophy. Because it must be understood by the masses, the language cannot be philosophically precise. The point of this argument is to again differentiate between what is accessible to the vulgar and what can be known by someone like Bruno, who has ascended the heavens and acquired godlike comprehension. The acrimony of comments by Torquato also provide an occasion to underscore the ignorance of England's scholars and to lament the pervasive lack of learning and manners.[7] This treatment, however, is tempered by the courtesy of the noblemen who have invited him.

> The gentlemen besought the Nolan not to be upset by the unkind incivility and rash ignorance of their doctors, but to pity the poverty of the country, which had been bereft of good scholarship, so far as members of the profession of philosophy and real mathematicians were concerned (and everyone being blind in these subjects, a pack of asses sell themselves as seers, and offer bladders as lanterns).... (193)

In the fifth dialogue Bruno further discusses his cosmology. He contends that the cosmos is infinite and argues that all motion is internal, a result of the earth and the other planets being alive. The eternal interchange and transmutation of the parts of the earth create the earth's motion and climatic variation. In this context, Bruno comments that this condition—an immortal earth with mortal constituents—accounts for decline and disease but also offers the hope for renewal and rebirth. The dialogue then concludes somewhat cryptically. Prudenzio asks Teofilo whether the flux will ever end, whether there will always be a need for restoration. Teofilo does not respond directly but says he will provide a copy of Bruno's dialogue *Purgatorio de l'inferno,* in which one may see the fruit of redemption. The dialogue is lost and its contents remain unknown. It is apparent, however, that it would address the question of perpetual flux and would point to the redemptive process in nature and religion. Some scholars have speculated that the dialogue *Spaccio della bestia trionfante* may be similar. That dialogue is certainly relevant to the theme and to our present concerns.

In *Spaccio della bestia trionfante (The Expulsion of the Triumphant Beast),* Bruno presents a brief mythic description of the end of an age of darkness and the beginning of enlightenment.[8] This text contains a scene in which the celestial powers that control the world convene to remedy the disorder that plagues it. In an elaborate mythic description of a realignment of planetary influences, the celestial powers are depicted as

---

7. Frulla, one of the participants, observes: "Such are the fruits of England; you can search far and wide, but you will find these days that all of them are professors of grammar, among whom, in this happy country, there reigns a constellation of the most obstinate pedantry, ignorance, and conceit, mingled with rustic rudeness that would try the patience of Job" (186). Frulla then comments on the rude treatment Bruno received at Oxford.

8. For an English translation, see *The Expulsion of the Triumphant Beast,* ed. and trans. A. D. Imerti (New Brunswick, N.J.: Rutgers University Press, 1964).

initiating this plan of action in order to renew or regenerate the creation. Following this description, Bruno comments that these efforts of the gods must be matched by the magus, who can use the new celestial alignments to help usher in the age of regeneration. This text makes it clear that the efforts of the magus are essential in overcoming human ignorance and in installing a perfect social order that will bring an end to the present state of turmoil.

In addition to searching the heavens for signs of a cosmic revitalization, Bruno also studied the political developments of his time in search of a leader who could pave the way for a universal religious and political reformation. Frances Yates has shown that some of Bruno's travels seem to have been aimed at facilitating some of these alignments. As already noted, he was drawn to England because of his high regard for the reign of Elizabeth, and there is reason to believe that he hoped she might be able to align herself with the French king, Henry III, to end the religious wars and bring some general political stability to Europe. When circumstances no longer favored Henry III, Bruno transferred his hopes to Henry of Navarre. In fact, according to Yates, it was Bruno's confidence that the accession of Henry IV would lead to a universal European religious and political reformation that prompted him to take the fatal step of returning to Italy.[9]

In the early 1590s, Bruno repeatedly expressed his conviction that he would be the spiritual messiah who would join with political leaders to affect a religious and political reformation. Part of the evidence of this comes in testimony from those in contact with him during this time. "The prior of the Carmelite monastery at which Bruno stayed in Frankfort . . . [reported] that he was always writing and dreaming and astrologising about new things . . . that he said that he knew more than the Apostles, and that, if he had a mind to it, he could bring it about that all the world should be of one religion."[10] When Henry of Navarre defeated the Catholic League and its Spanish backing in 1591, Bruno expected a "universal reform within a Catholic framework." This expectation was reported by an informant testifying against him at the Venetian Inquisition: "[Catholic religion] has need of great reform; it is not good as it is now, but soon the world will see a general reform of itself, for it is impossible that such corruptions should endure; he [Bruno] hopes great things of the King of Navarre, and he means to hurry to publish his works to gain credit in this way, for when the time comes he wishes to be

---

9. Yates, *Giordano Bruno*, 369.
10. Ibid., 340.

'capitano' and he will not be always poor for he will enjoy the treasures of others." Drawing upon the *Sommario* documents of his trial, Yates demonstrates that "the legend that Bruno was prosecuted as a philosophical thinker, was burned for his daring views on innumerable worlds or on the movement of the earth, can no longer stand."[11] It is now clear that Bruno was condemned for his belief that the Egyptian religion was the highest religion given by God, reversing the view of Ficino and others that the ancient theology pointed the way to the fuller revelation of Christianity. Moreover, his later years make clear that he understood his mission as one of a religious reformer who would be an instrument in the purging of the Church and in the institution of a new ecumenic religion based on Hermeticism and magic.

We have, then, in Bruno a further demonstration of the mounting criticism of orthodox Christianity and the concurrent turning toward the *prisca theologia* for the means of overcoming alienation and installing an enduring political order. Another important figure in perpetuating the vision of a utopian order founded on the principles of Hermeticism and magic is Campanella.

Tommaso Campanella

The year 1600, because of its numerological combinations of nine and three, signaled for Campanella the beginning of a new age in which the world would be renewed and religious strife and political turmoil put to an end. Like Bruno, Campanella found the key to understanding the new age in the Hermetic magical teachings. Like Bruno, he also believed he had a messianic role in ushering it in. In 1599 Campanella attempted to establish a new capital for worldwide religious and political reform at Calabria in southern Italy. This effort at rebellion against the Spanish monarchy and the papacy led to an imprisonment that cost twenty-five years of his life. It did not, however, destroy his dream of the renewal of society and the world, nor did it diminish his conviction that he was to play a signal role in bringing on this new age of light. While in prison Campanella wrote *The City of the Sun* (*La Città del Sole*), for which he is best remembered. During this time he also wrote to the Spanish monarch and then to the Pope describing the "natural" signs foretelling their destinies as leaders of a universal reform that would end the present state of ignorance and alienation.

Upon his release from prison, Campanella went to Rome and was well received by Pope Urban VIII and was even credited with performing astral magic that overcame the hostile configuration threatening the Pope's

---

11. Ibid., 355.

life. Shortly afterward, he went to France, where he was also well received by Louis XIII and Richelieu because he proclaimed that the French monarchy was to lead the reformation of the world. We will now look briefly at Campanella's writings and actions during the critical periods of the Calabrian revolt, the imprisonment, and his journeys to Rome and France following his release.

Campanella made little or no tactical preparation for his Calabrian revolt and gave little consideration to military strategies. Instead, he and his followers, many of whom were Dominican like him, attempted to prepare their countrymen by explaining signs that revealed a divinely inspired revolution which was to occur. Through his esoteric studies, Campanella found signs in the heavens for this revolution, particularly in the expectation that the sun was moving closer to the earth and in the numerological significance of the year 1600 already mentioned. After pointing to these signs, Campanella urged his listeners to become catalysts for the onset of the new age by freeing themselves from Spanish domination and by installing Campanella as the religious and political leader of the new era. *The City of the Sun*, which was written during his prison years, is not a utopia in the often used sense of an idealized, imaginary place free of the problems that plague the real world. It is now clear that it is a description of the state that Campanella had expected to establish in Calabria.

According to the text, the city was built on a hill surrounded by a vast plain. It was separated into seven circular divisions corresponding to the seven planets. Four roads crossed the city and followed the points of the compass, running from the outer gates to its center. At the very center of the city was a marvelous temple, an *omphalos* linking the city and the celestial powers that governed it. On the altar of the temple was a chart depicting the heavens and a map showing the earth. The ceiling of the dome displayed the great stars of heaven and the powers they have over things below. The temple also contained seven lamps named after the seven planets. The walls surrounding the temple were decorated on both sides to create an encyclopedia of accumulated mathematical, geographical, sociological, and philological records of the structure of the world and of its peoples. There were also descriptions of geological formations, the vegetative world, and the animal world. The mechanical arts and their inventors were displayed on the interior surface of the outermost wall, and on the outer surface were images of the inventors of sciences and laws, including Moses, Osiris, Jupiter, Mercury, Mohammed, and many others. In a high place of honor on this wall were Christ and the twelve apostles.[12] As Frances Yates rightly notes, "The City was thus a

---

12. This is a summary of *La Città del Sole: Diaglo Poetico*, trans. Daniel J. Donno

12. This is a summary of *La Città del Sole: Diaglo Poetico*, trans. Daniel J. Donn (Berkeley: University of California Press, 1981), 20–30.

complete reflection of the world as governed by the laws of natural magic in dependence on the stars. The great men were those who had best understood and used those laws, inventors, moral teachers, miracle workers, religious leaders, in short, Magi, of whom the chief was Christ with His apostles."[13] The head of the city was a priest-king, a master of natural magic. Through his administration

> the people of the City lived in brotherly love, having all things in common; they were intelligent and well-educated, the children beginning at an early age to learn all about the world and all arts and sciences from the pictures on the walls. They encouraged scientific invention, all inventions being used in the service of the community to improve the general well-being. They were healthy and well skilled in medicine. And they were virtuous. In this City, the virtues had conquered the vices, for the names of its magistrates were Liberality, Magnanimity, Chastity, Fortitude, Justice. . . . Hence, among the Solarians, there was no robbery, murder, incest, adultery, no malignity or malevolence of any kind.[14]

During his imprisonment Campanella also prepared *Monarchia di Spagna* and *Monarchia Messiae,* two works that prophesied the coming of a universal reform through either the Spanish monarchy or the papacy. This restless searching for a political leader grew out of Campanella's conviction that a new age was coming and that an ecumenic empire would be reestablished. Moreover, he continued to see this reform coming through a strengthening of Christianity by Hermetic magic, and he saw his own role as that of the primary shaper of the reform program. In each instance prophecy would be a reform "in which a priesthood of Catholic Magi keep the City in permanent happiness, health and virtue, and the religion of the City is in perfect accord with its scientific view of the world, that is to say with natural magic."[15] Frances Yates aptly describes the consequences of Campanella's efforts: "Campanella's astounding determination and pertinacity gradually had their reward; the monarchs of the world began to take an interest in the prisoner, and the man who, in 1599, had gone into prison in imminent danger of death for dangerous heresies and revolt against Spain was, in 1626, released from prison through Spanish influence."[16]

Two episodes in Campanella's career following his release deserve special attention. The first is the episode in which Campanella performed

---

13. Yates, *Giordano Bruno,* 369.
14. Ibid.
15. Ibid., 386.
16. Ibid., 387.

anti-eclipse magic for Pope Urban VIII.[17] Urban VIII, a firm believer in astrology, was greatly troubled by astrological forecasts predicting his imminent death. By 1628 rumors of his fate were widespread, no doubt encouraged by the Spanish, who were annoyed by his consistently pro-French policy. The two dangerous years were 1628, when there was an eclipse of the moon in January and of the sun in December, and 1630, when there was another solar eclipse in June. There are records showing that the Pope and Campanella frequently conferred on the meanings of these astrological events and the measures that could be taken against them. Campanella's own records indicate that he constructed what was in effect a model of the cosmos that could draw the beneficial powers from appropriate planets, thereby correcting the misalignment in the heavens. These efforts on behalf of the Pope gained Campanella sufficient favor that he was given permission to establish a college in Rome for the training of missionaries who would convert the whole world to Campanella's kind of Catholicism.[18]

By 1634, however, Campanella was again out of favor. Undaunted, he transferred his ministrations to the French monarchy. Shortly after his arrival in Paris, Campanella circulated his analysis of the astrological evidence showing that the power of the Spanish monarchy was weakening while that of the French monarchy was growing. In fact, Louis XIII was to be the new Charlemagne who would free Europe from Spanish tyranny. Moreover, the Paris edition of *The City of the Sun* linked Campanella's vision of utopian reform directly to the French monarchy. The most intriguing episode during his stay in France occurred in 1638, when Louis XIII's son was born. Campanella prepared an eclogue to commemorate the occasion. The eclogue was consistent with his vision of the French monarchy's restoration of universal harmony and was modeled after the famous messianic *Fourth Eclogue* of Virgil. Campanella's *Eclogue* opens in a fashion similar to the proclamation made to herald the Calabrian revolt—astrological signs show that a renewal of the world is at hand and that a new reign of religious vitality and social tranquility is about to begin. Campanella then refers to the Dauphin as the "French Cock destined to rule with a reformed Peter a united world. In this coming dispensation, labour will be a pleasure amicably shared by all; all will recognize one God and Father and love will unite all; all kings and peoples will assemble in a city which they will call Héliaca, the

---

17. See D. P. Walker, *Spiritual and Demonic Magic from Ficino to Campanella* (1958; reprint, South Bend, Ind.: University of Notre Dame Press, 1975), 205–12.
18. Campanella soon fell out of favor and the college was never begun.

City of the Sun, which will be built by this illustrious hero."[19] It is possible that Louis XIV gains the title "le roi Soleil" from this eclogue.

These events in Rome and in Paris in the last part of Campanella's life mark the full emergence of the Hermetic program of magical reform. In the Hermetic materials themselves and in Ficino's description of the powers of man as a terrestrial god, man is presented as a master of the forces that shape his destiny. In the account of the prophylactic magic Campanella performs on behalf of Urban VIII, we see a magus using his knowledge not only to draw beneficial powers from the heavens, but to create an alternate model that can correct a disorder in the heavens. With Campanella, too, the emphasis on the magus as the creator of a perfect social order emerges completely. As we saw in chapter 2, this is a fundamental element of the Hermetic materials. In the idealized city of Hermes, all human physical, emotional, and spiritual needs are met through the efforts of the magus. Campanella's efforts, similarly, are directed at the institution, or more accurately, the reinstitution of a perfect society.

Examination of Francis Bacon's writings will show that he shares Bruno's and Campanella's utopian views of social reformation through the recovery of knowledge permitting the mastery of nature.

---

19. Yates, *Giordano Bruno*, 390.

7. Francis Bacon: Ancient Wisdom and Utopian Reform

Bacon's reputation in the eighteenth and nineteenth centuries as a patriarch of science and a great field general in the battle of the ancients and moderns is certainly understandable. More than any other seventeenth-century thinker, he led the attack on traditional learning and made a thorough overhaul of the premises of philosophical and scientific inquiry. In addition to his theoretical work, he helped create a new scientific society (the Royal Society) to advance the understanding of the natural world and enhance the development of technology and the mechanical arts. Moreover, in laying the groundwork for a new form of scholarly collaboration, he set forth some of the most basic guidelines for scientific research, such as the sharing of theories and experimental results on an international basis and the testing of theories through independent experimental verification.

There are also many passages in Bacon's writings that link the advancement of a new learning to the prospects of a utopian social order. Bacon makes it clear that, for the new learning to serve as a basis for progress, it is necessary to tear down and clear away the clutter of the present educational system. And there is, as Blumenberg points out, Bacon's emphasis on knowledge as power and on the extraordinary developments in applied science that were opening new frontiers and expanding the horizons beyond anything conceived by the ancients.

For Blumenberg the "frontispiece" of Bacon's *The Great Instauration* is emblematic of the new epochal consciousness. Its depiction of a ship sailing beyond the Pillars of Hercules symbolizes the expansion and discovery underway since the fifteenth century that opened horizons beyond any imagined in previous times. This image also has a mythical significance as well. In the ancient world the Pillars of Hercules marked the boundaries between the known, familiar world of man and the forbidden and treacherous ocean (*okeanos*) beyond man's knowledge or grasp. This symbolic representation of the familiar, habitable world and the unfamiliar and treacherous realm beyond complemented the concept of the ancient cosmos in which man had a definite place in the order of things. Knowledge in this conception depended on the discovery of the boundaries of man's nature so he did not fall into a tragic life of wanton and animalic behavior or of sinful pride that caused him to overstep his bounds and come into conflict with the gods. In fact, the Greek word often translated as *fate* derives from the term *moira* whose primary meaning is that of a boundary or an allotted portion. In this construction, knowledge is knowledge of one's place in the hierarchy of things, and exceeding such limits is symptomatic of ignorance, error, or sin. Bacon's image fundamentally transforms that ancient mythic understanding. It portrays the new man heroically sailing beyond the confines that had limited other generations to unnaturally constrained existence. By sailing beyond those boundaries, modern man transcends the barriers that had withheld him from what he could be, and he symbolically enters into the domain of higher beings.

Although an emphasis on advances in learning is an obvious and important element of Bacon's thought, Charles Whitney argues that it has been taken out of context and that a distorted picture of Bacon has therefore emerged.[1] This distortion has led, in turn, to a distorted understanding of modernity. Whitney's effort to open the perspective on Bacon and modernity centers on a reconsideration of the root symbols in Bacon's major works, the principal one being instauration. Whitney contends that Blumenberg's partial reading is due in great part to his effort to legitimize the modern age, to extricate it from accusations by Löwith and others that modern epochal themes derive from appropriated religious categories. Whitney's contention is that religious language, particularly the language of prophesy and apocalypse, permeated Bacon's age and that it supplied the root symbols and historical pattern at the core of modern epochal consciousness. After briefly developing Whitney's thesis, I will examine the relation of the *prisca theologia* to the prophetic and apocalyptic imagery that Whitney identifies by showing their presence in Bacon's writings. It should be immediately pointed out that the purpose of this analysis is not to attempt to transform Bacon from a scientist to a magician. Rather, it is to show the extent to which *prisca theologia* themes are part of the *zeitgeist* of Bacon's age.

For Whitney, Blumenberg's effort to make Bacon fit a stereotype requires him to discount the importance of the religious language that permeates Bacon's writings. According to Blumenberg, Bacon's religious language is a matter of pragmatic necessity as he attempts to persuade King James I to undertake reforms, but they are only the husk that surrounds the kernel of Bacon's project. The call for a new learning, the

---

1. Charles Whitney, *Francis Bacon and Modernity* (New Haven: Yale University Press, 1986).

linking of knowledge with power, and the urging of man to regain dominion over the world form the kernel of what is truly modern. In opposition to this view, Whitney develops a lengthy analysis of the central term *instauration* as it applies in Bacon's work. In an important essay in the *Journal of the History of Ideas,* Whitney has shown that the term had wide general usage from the ancient period up to Bacon's time.[2] The most important context for the term as Bacon uses it, however, is in the Vulgate edition of the account of the instauration of the Temple of Solomon during the time of King Josiah. During the reign of Solomon (1000 B.C.), the Hebrews enjoyed unprecedented prosperity and freedom from religious or political interference by neighboring powers in the Ancient Near East. After Solomon, however, the Hebrew nation was overrun and lost its political autonomy and religious freedom. In 624 B.C. pressure from neighboring powers waned and the young king Josiah was able to institute political and religious reforms, including the rebuilding of the temple. During reconstruction, the temple's Mosaic law code (the Deuteronomic Code) was rediscovered, and this was understood to be the beginning of a renewed covenant with God.

The specific context for this symbol is important for a number of reasons:

1. The instauration of the temple is a religious reform as well as a political reform, and as subsequent analysis will show, Bacon links the rebuilding of political and religious order to a rebuilding of nature.

2. The reference to Solomon has a poignancy in Bacon's time because King James referred to himself as the new Solomon who would bring the new Jerusalem, a primary motif in his coronation ceremonies.

3. Bacon was evidently hoping to emulate for King James the role of Josiah's chancellor, who urged the king to the reform and provided him the means for accomplishing it.

4. The rebuilding of the temple by Josiah represents the dual action of innovation and recovery. In order to build the new edifice, it was necessary to tear down the damaged structure. So the building of the temple is a new endeavor that can only be accomplished by clearing away what has existed. At the same time, however, the intent is to rebuild something that had existed before. At the symbolic level, the attempt involves creating in the present a more perfect rendering of the eternal ideal. As we shall see, this theme is connected to Bacon's view that modern knowledge is a recovery and an advance beyond ancient truth.

5. The image of renewal and reformation of the temple contains a clue

---

2. Whitney, "Bacon's *Instauratio,*" *Journal of the History of Ideas* 50 (1989), 371-90.

to other writings of Bacon in which he proposes or describes the restoration of man to his condition prior to the fall. Blumenberg himself devoted attention to Bacon's unorthodox interpretation of man's original sin. Bacon agrees with the biblical text that the original sin was an attempt to gain knowledge that God had denied mankind. He contends, however, that the sin is an attempt to gain knowledge of ethics or morality that is tied to salvation. The knowledge of salvation is different from the knowledge of nature that God had given man in order that he might have dominion over the world. Bacon therefore argues that a confusion over the nature of sin and the limits of human knowledge has left man unnecessarily enervated. God had intended man to know the cosmos and have dominion over the world. This distinction is found in other writings in which Bacon wants to separate religion from the arts and sciences, which are concerned with knowledge of the world.

6. The theme of instauration also occurs in Bacon's description of the rebuilding of the temple of knowledge. Passages in the *Advancement of Learning* offer sharp criticism of the present state of knowledge and call for a radical building that will open up avenues never known before. But in those same passages there is a reference to throwing off the present corrupt state of affairs so that the ancient truths can reemerge.

The points enumerated above anticipate thematic connections between Bacon's works and the emphasis on utopian reform through the Ancient Wisdom in the works of Agrippa, Bruno, and Campanella. The criticism of metaphysics and theology and the call for an abandoning of the vanities of knowledge (Bacon presents himself as a humble person reattuning himself to the natural world) are reminiscent of Agrippa's condemnation of the present state of learning. Bacon's argument for an abandonment of the false traditions of learning in order to discover deeper levels of truth also has a general connection with the theme of the *prisca theologia* tradition. More direct connections can also be made. There is, for instance, the remythologizing of pre-Adamite existence pointed to by Blumenberg. This reinterpretation of the biblical myth has close parallels to the myth in the *Corpus Hermeticum*. Bacon wants to underscore the God-given right to dominate the world and to possess godlike knowledge of the natural world. Another key connection is the emphasis on the House of Solomon or the Temple of Solomon in the *New Atlantis*. Whitney is right to connect it with the biblical tradition and to the circumstances regarding James I. But the Solomon of the *New Atlantis* also knew the secrets of nature and had a reputation for wisdom like that of the magus.

While the sustained reference to Solomon occurs in the *New Atlantis,* there are several passages in other works in which Bacon identifies

James I with the great ancient kings Solomon or Hermes Trismegistus or with the magus-kings of Persia. Therefore, before looking at the pertinent sections in the *New Atlantis*, let us look briefly at the references from the other works in which Bacon connects ancient knowledge with political and religious order. An important one occurs in the first book of the *Advancement of Learning* (1605). The theme of this work is that knowledge has become stagnant and that a wholesale reorientation of knowledge is required. This work is dedicated to James I in the hopes that he will recognize in Bacon's program a source for thoroughly reordering religion and politics. Bacon praises James and compares him to the greatest rulers of history. In the opening paragraphs, he praises James's learning as the source of his greatness: "[T]here is met in your Majesty a rare conjunction as well of divine and sacred literature as of profane and human; so as your Majesty standeth invested of that triplicity which in great veneration was ascribed to the ancient Hermes; the power and fortune of a King, the knowledge and illumination of a Priest, and the learning and universality of a Philosopher."[3] This reference recalls Ficino's explanation of Hermes' title. He is called "Trismegistus" because he was the greatest theologian, philosopher, and king. It is also reminiscent of Bruno's conviction that right knowledge is the key to a complete reordering of society and religion.

Obviously, too much should not be made of simple reference. On the other hand, its appearance in this work cannot be casual or unintended. Bacon has too much at stake in his petition not to have chosen his words and allusions carefully. It must be assumed, therefore, that James would find the comparison to Hermes flattering, just as he would the references to Solomon. Moreover, the allusion is evidently intended to indicate to the king the benefits of Bacon's project for the advancement of learning: it is connected directly to knowledge that enables a king to attain the greatness of the most venerated ruler in history.

If this were the only reference to Hermes or the *prisca theologia*, it would have minimal significance, even though it appears in a strategic work. There are parallel instances in other key works, however, and they reinforce the connections made here. In a masque for King James I, Bacon again refers to ancient kings who possessed knowledge and had great wisemen to help them rule. These passages occur as a counselor advises the king on the proper study of philosophy, urging him to use knowledge rather than force to rule.

---

3. *The Philosophical Works of Francis Bacon*, ed. John M. Robertson (1905; reprint, Freeport, N.Y.: Books for Libraries Press, 1970), 43.

I . . . will wish unto your Highness the exercise of the best and purest part of the mind, and the most innocent and meriting conquest, being the conquest of the works of nature . . . [by] searching out, inventing, and discovering of all whatsoever is hid and secret in the world; . . . Antiquity, that presenteth unto us in dark visions the wisdom of former times, informeth us that the [governments of] kingdoms have always had an affinity with the secrets and mysteries of learning. Amongst the Persians, the kings were attended on by the Magi. The Gymnosophists had all the government under the princes of Asia; and generally those kingdoms were accounted most happy, that had rulers most addicted to philosophy.[4]

The counselor then advises the King to devote himself to acquiring four aids to learning: (1) "a most perfect and general library," (2) an extensive garden of all plants and animals, (3) a huge cabinet of "whatsoever the hand of man by exquisite art or engine hath made," and (4) a "stillhouse, so furnished with mills, instruments, furnaces, and vessels, as may be a palace fit for a philosopher's stone." The four areas suggested here, the study of which Bacon equates with the acquisition and perfection of knowledge, are similar to the applied and technical arts that he advocates in the *Advancement of Learning* and the *Novum Organum* (1620). But this new philosophy is connected to the ancient knowledge of the kings and the magi, and its import extends beyond natural science. We have already noted the reference preceding the program of learning that links it to political and religious order. Immediately after the program is another comparison of James with Hermes: "Thus, when your Excellency shall have added depth of knowledge to the fineness of [your] spirits and greatness of your power, then indeed shall you be a Trismegistus; and then when all other miracles and wonders shall cease by reason that you shall have discovered their natural causes, yourself shall be left the only miracle and wonder of the world."[5]

Another text that makes similar connections between ancient knowledge of nature and knowledge of government is "A Brief Discourse Touching the Happy Union of the Kingdoms of England and Scotland" (1603). The private dedication begins:

> I do not find it strange (excellent King) that when Heraclitus, he that was surnamed the obscure, had set forth a certain book which is not now extant, many men took it for a discourse of nature, and many others took it for a treatise of policy and matter of estate. For there is a great affinity

---

4. Bacon, *Works*. 14 vols., ed James Spedding, R. L. Ellis, and D. D. Heath (1857–1874; reprint, Stuttgart: Friedrich Frommann, 1963), 8:334 (brackets in original).
5. Bacon, *Works,* 8:335 (brackets in original).

and consent between the rules of nature, and the true rules of policy: the one being nothing else but an order in the government of the world, and the other an order in the government of an estate. And therefore the education and erudition of the kings of Persia was in a science which was termed by a name then of great reverence, but now degenerate and taken in ill part: for the Persian magic, which was the secret literature of their kings, was an observation of the contemplations of nature and an application thereof to a sense politic; taking the fundamental laws of nature, with the branches and passages of them, as an original and first model, whence to take and describe a copy and imitation for government.[6]

Bacon then proposes a union of England and Scotland and urges that it be a true and harmonious union rather than a forced one. He uses alchemical references to set forth the kind of union needed, and it is evident that this is an example of the integration of nature and politics referred to in the other writings.

Another reference to Persian magic occurs in a later work, *De . . . augmentis scientiarum* (1623), the expanded Latin version of the *Advancement of Learning* (1605). Here the context is a discussion of the accuracy and adequacy of various forms of natural philosophy. Here Bacon distinguishes "popular and degenerate" natural magic from the ancient magic of the Persians, in order that the latter "be again restored to its ancient and honourable meaning." For among Persians "magic was taken for a sublime wisdom, and the knowledge of the universal consent of things; and so the three kings who came from the east to worship Christ were called by the name of Magi."[7]

If we now turn to the *New Atlantis* (1627), we are better prepared to understand the structure and the intent of Bacon's utopia. The *New Atlantis* is an account of the adventures of a group of Europeans who become shipwrecked on an uncharted island. New Atlantis's ability to meet the material needs of its people and to create prosperity, contentment, and well-being stand in sharp contrast to the deprivation and the religious and political turmoil of Europe. The Europeans are therefore anxious to know the reasons for the remarkable conditions in Ben Salem.

The information they want is provided during a series of interviews with a governor at the House of Strangers. The Europeans ask how the remote land came to be Christian and are told that some twenty years after the ascension of Christ, people on the eastern coast saw a pillar of light about a mile out at sea, on top of which was a "large cross of light, more bright and resplendent than the body of the pillar." When the

---

6. Ibid., 10:90.
7. Bacon, *Philosophical Works*, 474.

inhabitants attempted to reach the pillar, they were stopped short, unable to get nearer than sixty yards. One of the boats, however, contained one of the wisemen from the House of Solomon, the "very eye of this kingdom." After attentively contemplating this pillar and cross, the wiseman offered a prayer: "Lord God of heaven and earth, thou hast vouchsafed of thy grace to those of our order, to know thy works of creation, and the secrets of them; and to discern . . . between divine miracles, works of nature, works of art, and impostures and illusions of all sorts . . . testify that this is a miracle and beseech thee to give the interpretation and use of this great sign." In answer to the prayer, "'the pillar and cross of light brake up . . . and there was nothing left to be seen but a small ark or chest of cedar.' In it the wiseman found a Book and a Letter. The Book contained all the books of the Old and New Testaments and 'some other books of the New Testament which were not at that time written.'" The letter contained a declaration that the people "where God shall ordain this ark to come to land" shall have given to them "salvation and peace and goodwill."[8]

One interesting detail here is that the conversion comes shortly after the time of Christ. It is therefore a pristine form of Christianity not distorted and corrupted like the European tradition. It is also significant that the pristine truth is revealed to a member of the House of Solomon, not to commoners. In fact, the account makes it clear that the uneducated are incapable of approaching the epiphany or of interpreting the revelatory experience. Given the key role that they play, we must look more closely at the wisemen in the House of Solomon; before doing so, however, two further observations about the epiphany should be made. The first has to do with the primary symbols of the pillar and the cross. In light of the subsequent transformation, there is little question that the pillar refers to the pillar of fire that guided the chosen people away from Egypt into the Promised Land. In addition to its religious significance, this symbol has a political meaning as well. Deliverance from Egypt is delivery from disorder and slavelike existence into a land of "peace and good will." The pillar is also linked to knowledge, because it leads the people to Mount Horeb/Sinai, where Moses spent forty days and nights in God's presence. The result was the Mosaic law and in the Cabalist tradition the instruction in the secrets of the world comparable to the knowledge of the magus. This is a point to be returned to later in the discussion. When the pillar is transformed, it becomes part of

---

8. Bacon, *Philosophical Works*, 716–17. Subsequent quotations from the *New Atlantis* are cited with page numbers in the text.

the ark containing the teachings of the Old and New Testaments and "some books not yet written." Prior to the building of the temple, the ark stood as the primary symbol of religious and political order, and the ark was to be enshrined in the temple. These images will be examined further after consideration of two other important passages in the *New Atlantis.*

The first passage occurs when the Europeans ask about the House of Solomon. This house was founded by the greatest king of Ben Salem, whose name was Solomona. Solomona had ruled about 1900 years before, during a time when navigation and other arts were much more widely known and practiced than they are at present. "Amongst the excellent acts of that king, one above all hath the pre-eminence. It was the erection and institution of an Order or Society which we call *Salomon's House;* the noblest foundation (as we think) that ever was upon the earth; and the lanthorn of this kingdom" (721). Though some misinformed people think it was named after the founder, it was really named after the Hebrew king who was famous (even in Europe) for his study of the works and creatures of God. Similarly, Salomon's House, also called the College of the Six Days Works, was devoted to finding out the true nature of all things.[9]

Near the last sections of the book, the Europeans speak directly with "one of the Fathers of Salomon's House," who explains the ends of the order, its preparations and instruments, the several tasks or vocations of its members, and the rites and ordinances it observes. "The End of our Foundation is the Knowledge of Causes, and secret notions of things; and the enlarging of the bounds of the Human Empires, to the effecting of all things possible" (726). The ordinances and rites celebrate or "reverently commemorate human inventions and their hymns and services laud and thank God for his marvellous works and implore his aid in turn its labors to good and holy use" (727).

Finally, brief mention must be made of the name of the country. Atlantis is the mythical country referred to by Plato, but Bacon gives it his own meaning as well. This occurs when the governor tells the Europeans the history of Ben Salem and the rest of the world that is either unknown or has been distorted in European accounts. According to the governor, Ben Salem's history dates to the ancient times when the great kings and their wisemen built beautiful cities and used their knowledge to explore the world. One of the greatest of these empires was Atlantis. A deluge, however, destroyed much of Atlantis and other great countries, and Ben

---

9. There are interesting parallels between the House of Solomon (Salomon) and the program of the *Advancement of Learning,* as well as similarities to Bacon's advice concerning learning in the masque to the King.

Salem was cut off from them and remains the only one of the great ancient countries to retain its scientific knowledge. The rest have lost that knowledge and hence have lost touch with Ben Salem.

Recalling an earlier, more advanced state of knowledge and of civilization is a theme that must now be pursued because Bacon, like Bruno, links advancement of knowledge with recovery and juxtaposes the present, degenerate state of philosophy to its pristine form. Bacon's conception is most concisely presented in the fable of Orpheus in *De sapientia veterum* (*Wisdom of the Ancients;* 1609). In the preface of this intriguing work, Bacon explains that ancient myths and fables contain in compact mythic or allegorical form important truths that have since been lost, obscured, or distorted. For Bacon, the story of Orpheus is the story of the decline of philosophy as it descends from the natural philosophy of the ancient wisemen to moral and civil philosophy and finally to a state of almost total disintegration.

In its pristine state the "singing of Orpheus is of two kinds; one to propitiate the infernal powers, the other to draw the wild beasts and the woods." The former is natural philosophy; the latter moral and civil philosophy. "For natural philosophy proposes to itself as its noblest work of all, nothing less than the restitution [*instauro*] and renovation of things corruptible, and (what is indeed the same thing in a lower degree) the conservation of bodies in the state in which they are, and the retardation of dissolution and putrefaction."[10] This notion that natural philosophy involves restitution is strikingly like Ficino's description of natural magic and the use of the world spirit to maintain and perfect nature and society. The effort, however, means arduous labor, and failure leads to frustration and to the adoption of the easier task—the management of human affairs through moral and civil philosophy.

> Then Philosophy finding that her great work is too much for her, in sorrowful mood, . . . turns to human affairs; and applying her powers of persuasion and eloquence to insinuate into men's minds the love of virtue and equity and peace, teaches the people to assemble and unite and take upon them the yoke of laws and submit to authority, and forget their ungoverned appetites, in listening and conforming to precepts and discipline. . . . (836)

This stage of philosophy remains stable for a time, but then men return to "the depraved conditions of their nature" and these perturbations put moral and civil laws to silence. "And if such troubles last, it is not long before letters also and philosophy are so torn in pieces that no traces of

---

10. Bacon, *Philosophical Works,* 835, 836. Subsequent quotations from *Wisdom of the Ancients* are cited with page numbers in the text.

them can be found but a few fragments, scattered here and there. . . ." When philosophy and civilization reach this low point, barbarism sets in and disorder prevails "until, according to the appointed vicissitude of things, they break out and issue forth again, perhaps among other nations, and not in the places where they were before" (836). This fable has interesting affinities with the "Lament" of Hermes in the *Asclepius,* which was examined in chapter 3. Hermes tells his son that a time will come when the utopian conditions he has established will be lost and barbarism will prevail. A significant difference occurs, however, in the description of the recovery. Hermes has been assured that Egypt will recover the glory of the age of Hermes. In Bacon's myth the recovery will occur "perhaps among other nations, and not in the places where they were before." Does this not imply that England will be the new Jerusalem or the new Adocentyn or the New Atlantis?

Another of these fables, "Prometheus; or the State of Man," merits attention here. The key point is how the fable relates the advancement of learning to the recovery of the Ancient Wisdom Bacon admired. The elements of the story pertinent to our consideration are these:

> Tradition says that Man was made by Prometheus, and made of clay; only that Prometheus took particles from different animals and mixed them in. He, desiring to benefit and protect his own work, and to be regarded not as the founder only but also as the amplifier and enlarger of the human race, stole up to heaven with a bundle of fennel-stalks in his hand, kindled them at the chariot of the sun, and so brought fire to the earth and presented it to mankind. (848)

Ironically, though they benefited immensely, men were not grateful; in fact, they complained to Jupiter about this act of impiety, and as a reward Jupiter not only allowed mankind to keep the stolen fire, but also granted human beings perpetual youth. Foolishly, however, the recipients of this wonderful gift put them on the back of an ass. "The ass on his way home, being troubled with extreme thirst, came to a fountain; but a serpent that was set to guard it, would not let him drink unless he gave in payment whatever that was that he carried on his back. The poor ass accepted the condition; and so for a mouthful of water the power of renewing youth was transferred from men to serpents" (848). After they had lost the prize, Prometheus made peace with mankind, but he did not forgive Jupiter. In an attempt at revenge, he tricked Jupiter with a deceitful sacrifice. When Jupiter discovered the trickery, he attempted to take his revenge by having Vulcan create Pandora and her infamous box containing all the mischiefs and calamities of the world. She tempted Prometheus to open it, but he cunningly declined. His impetuous brother Epimetheus did, however, fall victim to the temptation and set evil loose on the world. Failing to fool Prometheus, Jupiter then decided to accuse him of many crimes, including the attempted rape of Minerva. As punishment, Prometheus is bound to Mount Caucasus, where an eagle perpetually feeds on his liver until he is rescued by Hercules. Eventually mankind comes to honor Prometheus, and "there were instituted in some nations games called torch-races, in which the runners carried lighted torches in their hands; and if any went out the bearer stood aside, leaving the victory to those that followed; and the first who reached the goal with his torch still burning received the prize" (849).

Bacon finds several truths on the surface and at the hidden depths of this allegory. For him, Prometheus represents Providence, "and the one thing singled out by the ancients as the special and peculiar work of Providence was the creation and constitution of Man." Providential creation imbues the nature of man with mind and intellect, which is "the seat of providence." The intent of this parable of man's nature "appears to be, that Man, if we look to final causes, may be regarded as the centre of the world; insomuch that if man were taken away from the world, the rest would seem to be all astray, without aim or purpose . . . and to be leading to nothing. For the whole world works together in the service of man; and there is nothing from which he does not derive use and fruit" (849). Bacon then offers a description of anthropocentric nature.

> The revolutions and courses of the stars serve him both for distinction of the seasons and distribution of the quarters of the world. . . . The winds sail his ships and work his mills and engines. Plants and animals of all kinds are made to furnish him either with dwelling and shelter or clothing or food or medicine, or to lighten his labour, or to give him pleasure and comfort; insomuch that all things seem to be going about man's business and not their own. Nor is it without meaning added that in the mass and composition of which man was made, particles taken from the different animals were infused and mixed up with the clay; for it is most true that of all things in the universe man is the most composite, so that he was not without reason called by the ancients the little world. . . . And this is indeed the reason it is capable of such wonderful powers and faculties. (849)

Prior to the gift from Prometheus, man was weak and helpless; fire, represents the mechanical arts and sciences that meet life's needs and improve the human condition.[11] The remarkable part of the parable for Bacon is the reaction of mankind to the gifts bestowed by the gods.

---

11. Fire is a symbol frequently associated with alchemy. Although Bacon is critical of corrupted forms of alchemy, he praises the pristine form.

The meaning of the allegory is, that the accusation and arraignment by men both of their own nature and of art, proceeds from an excellent condition of mind and issues in good; whereas the contrary is hated by the gods, and unlucky. For they who extravagantly extol human nature as it is and the arts as received; who spend themselves in admiration of what they already possess, and hold up as perfect the sciences which are professed and cultivated; are wanting, first, in reverence to the divine nature, with the perfection of which they almost presume to compare, and next in usefulness towards man; as thinking that they have already reached the summit of things and finished their work, and therefore need seek no further. They on the other hand who arraign and accuse nature and the arts, and abound with complainings are not only more modest . . . but are also stimulated perpetually to fresh industry and new discoveries. (850)

Understanding this truth shows that the wrong part of Greek philosophy has been revered. It should not be "confident and dogmatical philosophy" of Aristotle and the Peripatetics that is revered, but rather that of Empedocles and Democritus, who complain "that all things are hidden away from us, that we know nothing, . . . that truth is drowned in deep wells." And, according to Bacon, the moral of this allegory is that "conceit of plenty is one of the principal causes of want" (850).

In commenting on Jupiter's gift of unfading youth and its subsequent loss through human foolishness, Bacon takes a position reminiscent of Ficino's in *De vita triplici*: "it seems to show that methods and medicines for the retardation of age and the prolongation of life were by the ancients not despaired of, but reckoned rather among those things which men once had and by sloth and negligence let slip, than among those which were wholly denied or never offered" (850). He identifies the lazy and slow-paced ass as experience and notes that it might have reached its goal had it not been for the accident of thirst (appetite for profit or ostentation). "For if a man would put himself fairly under the command of experience, and proceed steadily onward by a certain law and method, and not let any thirst for experiments either of profit or ostentation seize him . . . such a man I do think would prove a carrier to whom new and augmented measures of divine bounty might be well enough entrusted" (851). Bacon then notes that the reconciliation of Prometheus with mankind contains an important truth. "It alludes to the levity and rashness of men in new experiments; who if an experiment does not at once succeed according to wish, are in far too great a hurry to give up the attempt as a failure, and so tumble back to where they were and take on with the old things again" (851).

In Bacon's interpretation Pandora represents the pleasure and sensual appetites accompanying the civil arts, which make luxury possible. The love of pleasure to which the impetuous (Epimetheus) fall victim is the source of "infinite mischief upon the minds, the bodies, and fortunes" of individuals and the cause of wars, civil disturbances, civil tyrannies in kingdoms and commonwealths. Prometheus's crime against Minerva, which resulted in "the tearing of his entrails," appears to be a crime caused by man's arrogant attempt to bring the divine wisdom under the dominion of sense and reason. In a passage reminiscent of his treatment of the fall of Adam, Bacon warns that "men must soberly and modestly distinguish between things divine and human, between the oracles of sense and of faith; unless they mean to have at once a heretical religion and a fabulous philosophy" (852).

The torch races in honor of Prometheus also allude to the arts and sciences and carry "a very wise admonition." The perfection of the sciences is not to be found in the ability of any single inquirer but necessitates a succession of effort: "therefore men should be advised to rouse themselves, and try each his own strength and the chance of his own turn, and not to stake the whole venture upon the spirits and brains of a few persons" (852–53). Through these collaborative efforts, the achievements of the ancients might be revived and advanced. "These races and games of the torch have long been intermitted; since it is still in their first authors . . . that we find the several sciences in highest perfection; and no great matter has been done, nor hardly attempted, by their successors" (852).

Now, having examined these materials, what common themes can be drawn from them? First of all, there is the obvious and well-established effort of Bacon to persuade the king that the advancement of knowledge is the key to his success as a great political, religious, and intellectual leader. This is the theme of the *New Atlantis,* in which the greatest of the kings of Ben Salem was Solomon, to whom James is compared. The text makes it abundantly clear that Solomon's singular achievement was the establishment of the House of Solomon, which developed the arts and sciences that met the needs of the country. This house carried out the activities described in the *Advancement of Learning* and the masque. It is also evident that the knowledge being provided was of the mechanical arts and sciences, not the metaphysical speculation that Bacon is so critical of in other contexts.

This kind of knowledge is at once ancient and new. According to the *New Atlantis,* Ben Salem's history dates back to the time of the great ancient civilizations that achieved remarkable advances in the arts and sciences. Natural calamities and warfare, however, destroyed the others and their histories have been lost or obscured. Only Ben Salem stands as testimony to the benefits that right knowledge is capable of providing the king and his country. The two fables in *De sapientia* contain a similar view. The myth of Orpheus explains that the highest philosophy is a natural philosophy which provides an understanding of the secrets of nature through which man can improve the human condition. Like the *New Atlantis,* however, the fable describes the degeneration of philosophy into an ineffectual moral and civil philosophy that is followed in turn by barbarianism. There is hope, however, because some fragments of the highest forms of ancient truth remain and, when properly interpreted, can be used to reestablish right knowledge. This theme also resides in the Prometheus fable, in which man's greatness is attained through the mechanical arts but the perfection of knowledge is then disrupted for millennia.

Now what is to be made of these various references? Do the allusion to Persian magic and Bacon's implicit identification with the role of the magus make him a magician? The answer is *no*. But the passages quoted here, which have been virtually ignored by Blumenberg and others, do substantially alter the understanding of Bacon and the origins of modern utopianism. Bacon, like Renaissance Neoplatonists and like Agrippa, Campanella, and Bruno, does view the present disorder as the result of an age of darkness produced by learned ignorance. Moreover, he also agrees that the knowledge to be recovered is like that of Hermes Trismegistus and other great intellectual, religious, and political leaders of the *prisca theologia*. That is, right knowledge is the knowledge of nature that permits the relief of mankind's state. There is an important difference, however, as the texts also make clear. Bacon is convinced that magic has been corrupted; as a result, its methods are faulty.[12] Science provides a better means to obtain the same ends (compare the methods praised in Bacon's interpretation of the torch races). Now, this shift is quite profound, but so is the continuity in the aims and goals of knowledge, which are related to political and religious order.

The new Atlantis is an image of a primordial or pristine condition existing before the world was corrupted by philosophy and theology. The restoration of Atlantis is a rebuilding of a secular city that is analogous to the rebuilding of the Temple of Solomon. It also parallels Bacon's call in his other writings for James to become the new Solomon, and the call to

---

12. Bacon discusses the decline of magic from its pure, original form in *Philosophical Works,* 474. He contrasts the occult methods of magic and alchemy to the new science in "The Masculine Birth of Time" (in Benjamin Farrington, *The Philosophy of Francis Bacon* [Chicago: University of Chicago Press, 1964], 70-71).

build the new temple further evokes James's identification with Solomon and the new Jerusalem. The *New Atlantis* offers him the blueprint of what is possible if he uses the new learning—which is also the old learning. It will take English society away from the ignorance and error that plagues Europe and create the conditions that existed before man became alienated and overwhelmed by erroneous interpretations of his finitude and his sin.

In the context of this discussion, it is important to underscore Whitney's argument that proving Bacon was a devout Christian is unnecessary in demonstrating the importance of the prophetic and apocalyptic imagery in his works. Similarly, it is not necessary to make Bacon a magus in order to demonstrate the influence of the *prisca theologia*. Just as there is a substantial body of scholarship that now details the prevalence of apocalyptic and millenarian imagery in Bacon's time, there is a growing body of scholarship that demonstrates the pervasiveness of Platonic, Hermetic, and Rosicrucian symbols in the sixteenth and seventeenth centuries.

These myths and symbols combine with apocalyptic and millenarian patterns to express an intense longing for a new age of enlightenment, rebirth, and instauration. The distinctive contribution of the *prisca theologia* to the modern epochal consciousness is in the emphasis on man's role in recovering or discovering knowledge and in his active use of knowledge to shape his destiny.

Conclusion

This study has been an attempt to establish a new approach to the origins of modern epochal consciousness by demonstrating the influence of the *prisca theologia* tradition, which was introduced into early modern thought as part of the Renaissance recovery of ancient learning. While this tradition is a widely divergent collection of esoteric religion and pseudo-science, Ficino and other Neoplatonic/Hermetic philosophers were drawn to its myths and symbols of enlightenment through knowledge and used them to develop an elaborate immanentist concept of man's relation to God and the world. Initially, this conception was seen as an augmentation of orthodox Christian thought. In the sixteenth and seventeenth centuries, however, it proved to be another source of criticism about the confusion and disorder plaguing Christendom. Agrippa, for example, understood the promise of a new age of light to depend on a recovery of the ancient teachings and on a rejection of the muddled state of Christian philosophy and theology. Similarly, Francis Bacon believed that the new utopian age depended on a rejection of established religious views of man's relation to God and to the world. Although his instrument for ushering in the new age was science and technology, the inspiration for his great instauration was a combination of Christian millenarianism and the *prisca theologia*.

To suggest that esoteric religious and pseudo-scientific images and symbols lie in the main lines of modern thought challenges, of course, the long-standing claims that it is an age of science and secularization. Although science and secularization are obviously major influences, they are not the only ones to contribute to the distinctive modern emphasis on knowledge as power and on man as the active shaper of his destiny. The Hermetic materials revived by Ficino contain precisely these themes, and historical analysis shows the path of their transmission into the mainstreams of modern thought. Moreover, it shows that the advocates of the Ancient Wisdom are also important proponents of the new science.

The analysis of this material's significance in understanding modern epochal consciousness was developed in comparison to the important work of Hans Blumenberg. Blumenberg was chosen because he also focuses on modernity's emphasis upon the human self-assertion and epochal progress that result from a new epistemology. Blumenberg also maintained that the modern epochal pattern can only be understood in relation to Christian efforts to resolve the dilemmas created by its ambivalent attitude to the world. The fundamental difference between Blumenberg's approach and the one taken here is that Blumenberg views modern self-assertion as a necessary consequence of the exhaustion of medieval religion. This study demonstrates, however, that orthodox and unorthodox religion influenced modern thought and modern historical interpretation long after the Scholastic-Nominalist clash has subsided. In fact, elements of these esoteric religious traditions shaped the modern age's utopian dream of controlling nature and perfecting society.

Bibliography

This bibliography is organized under three main topics: (1) Blumenberg: Secularization, Gnosticism, and Modernity; (2) the *Prisca Theologia* and Renaissance Theology; and (3) the *Prisca Theologia* and Utopian Reform. Each of these topics has been broken into three subdivisions, and these groupings are explained at the beginning of each main section.

Blumenberg: Secularization, Gnosticism, and Modernity

This section includes primary and secondary sources for Blumenberg's work, studies of the concept of secularization and its relation to modernity, and primary and secondary sources for ancient and modern Gnosticism.

Blumenberg

Baskin, William. Review of *The Legitimacy of the Modern Age*, by Hans Blumenberg. *Religious Studies Review* 11 (April 1985): 165-70.

Blumenberg, Hans. *The Genesis of the Copernican World*. Translated by Robert M. Wallace. Cambridge, Mass.: MIT Press, 1987. Originally published as *Die Genesis der kopernikanischen Welt* (Frankfurt; Suhrkamp, 1975).

———. *Das Lachen der Thrakerin: Eine Urgeschichte der Theorie*. Frankfurt am Main: Suhrkamp, 1987.

———. *The Legitimacy of the Modern Age*. Translated by Robert M. Wallace. Cambridge, Mass.: MIT Press, 1983. Originally published as *Die Legitimität der Neuzeit* (Frankfurt: Suhrkamp Verlag, 1976).

———. "On a Lineage of the Idea of Progress." Translated by E. B. Ashton. *Social Research* 41 (Spring 1974): 5-27.

———. *Work on Myth*. Translated by Robert M. Wallace. Cambridge, Mass.: MIT Press, 1985. Originally published as *Arbeit am Mythos* (Frankfurt: Suhrkamp, 1979).

Bouwsma, William J. Review of *The Legitimacy of the Modern Age*, by Hans Blumenberg. *Journal of Modern History* 56 (1984): 698-701.

———. "Work on Blumenberg." Review of *Work on Myth*, by Hans Blumenberg. *Journal of the History of Ideas* 48 (1987): 347-54.

Crosson, Frederick J. "Modernity's Non-Christian Origins." Review of

The Legitimacy of the Modern Age, by Hans Blumenberg. *Review of Politics* 47 (1985): 625-28.

Faber, Richard. "The Rejection of Political Theology: A Critique of Hans Blumenberg." Translated by David J. Parent. *Telos* 72 (1987): 173-86.

Gadamer, H. G. Review of *Die Legitimität der Neuzeit*, by Hans Blumenberg. *Philosophische Rundschau* 15 (1968): 201-9.

Harries, Karsten. "Copernican Reflections." Review of *Die Genesis der kopernikanischen Welt*, by Hans Blumenberg. *Inquiry* 23 (1980): 253-69.

Jay, Martin. Review of *The Legitimacy of the Modern Age*, by Hans Blumenberg. *History and Theory* 24 (1985): 183-96.

Kalin, Martin G. Review of *Die Genesis der kopernikanischen Welt*, by Hans Blumenberg. *Contemporary German Philosophy* 1 (1982): 243-52.

Löwith, Karl. Review of *Die Legitimität der Neuzeit*, by Hans Blumenberg. *Philosophische Rundschau* 15 (1968): 195-201.

McKnight, Stephen A. "The Legitimacy of the Modern Age: The Löwith-Blumenberg Debate in Light of Recent Scholarship." *The Political Science Reviewer* 19 (1990): 177-95.

Pannenberg, Wolfhart. "Christianity as the Legitimacy of the Modern Age: Thoughts on a Book by Hans Blumenberg." Translated by George H. Kehm. In *Basic Questions in Theology*. 3 vols. (London: SCM Press, 1973), 3:178-219.

Pippin, Robert B. "Blumenberg and the Modernity Problem." *The Review of Metaphysics* 40 (March 1987): 535-57.

Wallace, Robert M. "Hans Blumenberg on Descartes and the Modern Age." *Annals of Scholarship* 5 (Fall 1987): 37-63.

———. "Introduction to Blumenberg." *New German Critique* 11 (Spring-Summer 1984): 93-108.

———. "Progress, Secularization, and Modernity: The Löwith-Blumenberg Debate." *New German Critique* 8 (Winter 1981): 63-79.

Yack, Bernard. "Myth and Modernity: Hans Blumenberg's Reconstruction of Modern Theory." *Political Theory* 15 (1987): 244-61.

Secularization and Modernity

Delekat, Friedrich. *Ueber den Begriff der Säkularisation*. Heidelberg: Quelle and Meyer, 1958.

Dickey, Laurence. "Blumenberg and Secularization: 'Self-Assertion' and the Problem of Self-Realizing Teleology in History." Review of *The Legitimacy of the Modern Age*, by Hans Blumenberg. *New German Critique* 14 (1987): 151-65.

Hübener, Wolfgang. "Carl Schmitt und Hans Blumenberg oder über Kette und Schuss in der historischen Textur der Moderne." In *Der Fürst dieser Welt. Carl Schmitt und die Folgen*, vol. 1 of *Religionstheorie und politische Theologie*, edited by J. Taubes. Munich: W. Fink, 1983.

Löwith, Karl. *Meaning in History: The Theological Implications of the Philosophy of History*. Chicago: University of Chicago Press, 1949.

———. *Weltgeschichte und Heilgeschehen: Die theologischen Voraussetzungen der Geschichtsphilosophie*. 2d ed. Stuttgart: Kohlhammer, 1953.

Lübbe, Hermann. *Säkularisierung: Geschichte eines ideenpolitischen Begriffs*. Freiburg: K. Alber, 1965.

Stallman, M. *Was ist Säkularisierung?* Tübingen: J. C. B. Mohr, 1960.

Gnosticism: Ancient and Modern

Aland, Barbara, ed. *Gnosis: Festschrift für Hans Jonas*. Göttingen: Vandenhoeck und Ruprecht, 1978.

Filoramo, G. *Gnosticism*. Translated by Anthony Alcock. Oxford: Basil Blackwell, 1990. Originally published as *L'attesa della fine: Storia della gnosi*.

Jonas, Hans. *Gnosis und spätantiker Geist*. 4th ed. 2 vols. Göttingen: Vandenhoeck und Ruprecht, 1988.

———. "Gnosticism." In *Encyclopedia of Philosophy* (New York: Macmillan, 1967).

———. *The Gnostic Religion: The Message of the Alien God and the Beginnings of Christianity*. 2d ed. Boston: Beacon Press, 1963.

Layton, Bentley, ed. *The Rediscovery of Gnosticism*. Proceedings of the International Conference on Gnosticism, Yale University, New Haven, Connecticut, March 28-31, 1978. 2 vols. Leiden: Brill, 1980, 1981 (supplements to *Numen* 41).

McKnight, Stephen A. "Understanding Modernity: A Reappraisal of the Gnostic Element." *Intercollegiate Review* 14 (1979): 107-17.

Pagels, Elaine. *The Gnostic Gospels*. New York: Random House, 1979.

Rudolph, Kurt. *Gnosis: The Nature and History of Gnosticism*. Edited by Robert McLachlan Wilson et al. San Francisco: Harper and Row, 1983.

Scholer, David M. "Bibliographica Gnostica: Supplementum I." *Novum Testamentum* 13 (1971): 322-36.

———. *Nag Hammadi Bibliography: 1948-1969*. Leiden: Brill, 1971.

Sebba, Gregor. "History, Modernity and Gnosticism." In *The Philosophy of Order: Essays on History, Consciousness and Politics*, edited by Peter J. Opitz and Gregor Sebba. Stuttgart: Klett-Cotta, 1981.

Taubes, Jacob, ed. *Gnosis und Politik*. Munich: W. Fink, 1984.
Tröger, Karl-Wolfgang. "Die hermetische Gnosis." In *Gnosis und Neues Testament*, edited by Karl-Wolfgang Tröger, 97–119. Berlin: Evangelische Verlagsanstalt, 1973.
Voegelin, Eric. *From Enlightenment to Revolution*. Durham, N.C.: Duke University Press, 1975.
———. *New Science of Politics*. Chicago: University of Chicago Press, 1952.
———. *Science, Politics and Gnosticism: Two Essays*. Chicago: H. Regnery, 1968.
Wilson, R. McL. *The Gnostic Problem*. 1958. Reprint. New York: AMS Press, 1980.

The *Prisca Theologia* and Renaissance Theology

This section contains primary and secondary sources for Ficino's writings, interpretive studies of Giotto, Michelangelo, and Botticelli, and primary sources and interpretive studies for the Ancient Wisdom and its influence on Renaissance thought.

Ficino

Bowen, William Roy. *Music and Number: An Introduction to Renaissance Harmonic Science*. Microform. Ottawa: National Library of Canada, 1985.
Cassirer, E. "Ficino's Place in Intellectual History." Review of *The Philosophy of Marsilio Ficino*, by Paul O. Kristeller. *Journal of the History of Ideas* 6 (1945): 483–501.
Clark, John R. "The Manuscript Tradition of Marsilio Ficino's 'De vita libri tres.'" *Manuscripta* 27 (November 1983): 158–64.
Copenhaver, Brian P. "Renaissance Magic and Neoplatonic Philosophy: 'Ennead' 4.3–5 in Ficino's 'De vita coelitus comparanda.'" In vol. 2 of *Marsilio Ficino e il ritorno di Platone*, edited by Gian Carlo Garfagnini. 2 vols. Florence: L. S. Olschki, 1986.
———. "Scholastic Philosophy and Renaissance Magic in the 'De vita' of Marsilio Ficino." *Renaissance Quarterly* 37 (Winter 1984): 523–54.
Ficino, Marsilio. *Opera Omnia*. 4 vols. 2d. ed. 1576. Reprint. Turin: Bottega d'Erasmo, 1959.
———. *Théologie Platonicienne de l'immortalité des âmes*. 3 vols. Translation and commentary by Raymond Marcel. Paris: Société d'édition "Les Belles Lettres," 1964–1970.
———. *Three Books on Life: A Critical Edition and Translation with Introduction and Notes*. Edited by Carol V. Kaske and John R. Clark.

Medieval and Renaissance Texts and Studies, vol. 57. Binghamton, N.Y.: Renaissance Society of America, 1989.
Field, Arthur M. *The Origins of the Platonic Academy of Florence.* Princeton, N.J.: Princeton University Press, 1988.
Gandillac M. De. "Neoplatonism and Christian Thought in the Fifteenth Century (Nicholas of Cusa and Marsilio Ficini)." In *Neoplatonism and Christian Thought,* edited by Dominic J. O'Meara. Albany, N.Y.: State University of New York Press, 1982.
Hersey, G. L. "Marsilio Ficino's Cosmic Temple." In *Collaboration in Italian Renaissance Art,* edited by Wendy Stedman Sheard and John T. Paoletti. New Haven, Conn.: Yale University Press, 1978.
Kaske, Carol. "Ficino's Shifting Attitude towards Astrology in the 'De vita coelitus comparanda,' the Letter to Poliziano, and the 'Apologia' to the Cardinals." In vol. 2 of *Marsilio Ficino e il ritorno di Platone: Studi e documenti,* edited by Gian Carlo Garfagnini. 2 vols. Florence: L. S. Olschki, 1986.
Klibansky, R., E. Panofsky, and F. Saxl. *Saturn and Melancholy: Studies in the History of Natural Philosophy, Religion and Art.* New York: Basic Books, 1964.
Kristeller, Paul Oskar. "Marsilio Ficino as a Beginning Student of Plato." *Scriptorium* 20 (1966): 41–54.
———. *The Philosophy of Marsilio Ficino.* Translated by Virginia Conant. New York: Columbia University Press, 1943.
Michel, Paul-Henri. "Renaissance Cosmologies." *Diogenes* 18 (Summer 1957): 93–107.
Mueller-Jahnke, W. D. "Von Ficino zu Agrippa, Der Magie-Begriff des renaissance-Humanismus im Ueberblick." In *Epochen der Naturmystik,* edited by A. Faivre and R. C. Zimmermann. Berlin: E. Schmidt, 1979.
Torre, Arnaldo della. *Storia dell'Accademia platonica di Firenze.* Florence: Tip. G. Carnesecchi e figli, 1902.
Trinkaus, Charles. *In Our Image and Likeness: Humanity and Divinity in Italian Humanist Thought.* 2 vols. Chicago: University of Chicago Press, 1970.
Warden, John. "Orpheus and Ficino." In *Orpheus: The Metamorphoses of a Myth,* edited by John Warden. Toronto: University of Toronto Press, 1982.
Zambelli, Paola. "Le problème de la magie naturelle à la Renaissance." In *Magia, astrologia e religione nel Rinascimento.* Wroclaw: Zaklad Narodowy im Ossolinskich, 1974.

Giotto, Michelangelo, and Botticelli

Battisti, Eugenio. *Giotto: A Biographical and Critical Study*. Translated by James Emmons and edited by Albert Skira. Vol. 32 of *The Taste of Our Time*. Lausanne: Skira, 1960.

Baxandall, Michael. *Giotto and the Orators: Humanist Observers of Painting in Italy and the Discovery of Pictorial Composition, 1350-1450*. Oxford: Clarendon Press, 1971.

Chastel, André. *Art et humanisme à Florence au temps de Laurent le Magnifique*. 2d ed. Paris: Presses universitaires de France, 1961.

Cox-Rearick, Janet. *Dynasty and Destiny in Medici Art: Pontormo, Leo X, and the Two Cosimos*. Princeton: Princeton University Press, 1984.

Dempsey, Charles. "'Mercurius Ver': The Sources of Botticelli's 'Primavera.'" *Journal of the Warburg and Courtauld Institutes* 31 (1968): 251-73.

Dixon, John. W., Jr. "The Christology of Michelangelo: The Sistine Chapel." *The Journal of the American Academy of Religion* 55 (1987): 503-33.

———. "Painting as Theological Thought: The Issues in Tuscan Theology." In *Humanities, Religion, and the Arts Tomorrow*, edited by Howard Hunter. New York: Holt, Rinehart and Winston, 1972.

Ettlinger, L. D., and Helen S. Ettlinger. *Botticelli*. New York: Oxford University Press, 1977.

Ferruolo, A. B. "Botticelli's Mythologies, Ficino's 'De Amore,' Poliziano's 'Stanze per la Giostra': Their Circle of Love." *Art Bulletin* 37 (1955): 17-25.

Gombrich, E. H. *Symbolic Images: Studies in the Art of the Renaissance*. Oxford: Phaidon, 1978.

Lightbown, Ronald. *Sandro Botticelli*. 2 vols. 2d ed. Berkeley: University of California Press, 1978.

———. *Sandro Botticelli: Life and Work*. New York: Abbeville Press, 1989-.

Panofsky, Erwin. *Meaning in the Visual Arts: Papers in and on Art History*. Garden City, N.Y.: Doubleday, 1955.

———. *Renaissance and Renascences in Western Art*. 2 vols. Stockholm: Almqvist and Wiksell, 1960.

———. *Studies in Iconology: Humanistic Themes in the Art of the Renaissance*. New York: Harper and Row, 1967.

Scardeone, Bernardino. *De antiquitate urbis Patavii et claris Civibus Patavinis*. Basel, 1560.

Seznec, Jean. *The Survival of the Pagan Gods: The Mythological Tradition and Its Place in Renaissance Humanism and Art.* New York: Harper and Row, 1953.
Stubblebine, James H., ed. *Giotto: The Arena Chapel Frescoes.* New York: Norton, 1969.
Tolnay, Charles de. *Michelangelo.* 6 vols. Princeton: Princeton University Press, 1969-1972.
Trexler, Richard C. "Florentine Religious Experience: The Sacred Image." *Studies in the Renaissance* 19 (1972): 7-41.
Wind, Edgar. *Pagan Mysteries in the Renaissance: An Exploration of Philosophical and Mystical Sources of Iconography in Renaissance Art.* 3d ed. Oxford: Oxford University Press, 1980.

Prisca Theologia

Apuleius. *The Isis-Book: (Metamorphoses, Book XI).* Edited and translated by J. Gwyn Griffiths. Leiden: Brill, 1975.
Betz, Hans Dieter. "The Delphic Maxim ['Know Thyself'] in Hermetic Interpretation." *Harvard Theological Review* 63 (October 1970): 465-84.
Blau, J. L. *The Christian Interpretation of the Cabala in the Renaissance.* Port Washington, N.Y.: Kennikat Press, 1944.
Couliano, Ioan P. *Eros and Magic in the Renaissance.* Chicago: University of Chicago Press, 1987.
Festugière, A. J. *La Révélation d'Hermès Trismégiste.* 4 vols. Paris: Librairie Lecoffre, 1949-1954.
Fowden, Garth. *The Egyptian Hermes: A Historical Approach to the Late Pagan Mind.* Cambridge: Cambridge University Press, 1986.
―――. "The Platonist Philosopher and His Circle in Late Antiquity." *Philosophia* 7 (1977): 359-83.
Fröbe-Kapteyn, Olga, ed. *Das hermetische Prinzip in Mythologie, Gnosis und Alchemie.* 2d ed. Vol. 9 of *Eranos Jahrbuch.* Zurich: Rhein-Verlag, 1967.
Garin, Eugenio. *Astrology in the Renaissance: The Zodiac of Life.* Translated by Carolyn Jackson and June Allen. Translation revised by Clare Robertson in collaboration with author. London: Routledge and Kegan Paul, 1983.
―――. *La Cultura filosofica del Rinascimento italiano: Ricerche e documenti.* Florence: Sansoni, 1961.
―――. "Magic and Astrology in the Civilisation of the Renaissance." Translated by Peter Munz. In *Science and Civic Life in the Italian Renaissance.* Garden City, N.Y.: Anchor Books, 1969.

———. *Medioevo e Rinascimento: Studi e ricerche.* 2d ed. Rome: Laterza, 1987.
———. *Testi umanistici su l'ermetismo.* Rome: Bocca, 1955.
Georgi, Dieter, and John Strugnell. *Concordance to the "Corpus Hermeticum": Tractate One: the "Poimandres."* Concordances to Patristic and Late Classical Texts, vol. 0. Cambridge, Mass.: Boston Theological Institute, 1971.
Gersh, Stephen. *Middle Platonism and Neoplatonism: The Latin Tradition.* 2 vols. Notre Dame: University of Notre Dame Press, 1986.
González Blanco, A. "Hermetism: A Bibliographical Approach." In *Aufstieg und Niedergang der romischen Welt*, edited by Hildegard Temporini. Part 2, vol. 17, no. 4. (Berlin: De Gruyter, 1984), 2240-81.
Grese, William C. *Corpus Hermeticum XIII and Early Christian Literature.* Leiden: Brill, 1979.
———. "The Hermetica and New Testament Research." *Biblical Research* 28 (1983): 37–54.
Gundel, H. "Poimandres." In *Paulys Real-Encyclopädie der Classischen Altertumswissenschaft.* New ed. Stuttgart-Waldsee: Alfred Druckenmüller Verlag, 1951.
Hersey, G. L. *Pythagorean Palaces: Magic and Architecture in the Italian Renaissance.* Ithaca: Cornell University Press, 1976.
Kerényi, Karl. *Hermes, Guide of Souls: The Mythologem of the Masculine Source of Life.* Translated by Murray Stein. Dallas: Spring Publications, 1986.
Luck, Georg, comp. and trans. *Arcana Mundi: Magic and the Occult in the Greek and Roman Worlds: A Collection of Ancient Texts.* Baltimore: Johns Hopkins University Press, 1985.
Merkel, Ingrid and Allen G. Debus, eds. *Hermeticism and the Renaissance: Intellectual History and the Occult in Early Modern Europe.* Washington, D.C.: Folger Shakespeare Library, 1988.
Moorsel, G. van. *The Mysteries of Hermes Trismegistus: A Phenomenologic Study in the Process of Spiritualisation in the Corpus Hermeticum and Latin Asclepius.* Utrecht, 1955.
Nock, A. D., and A. J. Festugière, trans. *Corpus Hermeticum.* 4 vols. Paris: Société d'édition "Les Belles Lettres," 1954–1960.
Reitzenstein, Richard. *Poimandres: Studien zur griechisch-ägyptischen und frühchristlichen Literatur.* Leipzig: B. G. Teubner, 1904.
Robb, Nesca A. *Neoplatonism of the Italian Renaissance.* 1935. Reprint. New York: Octagon Books, 1968.
Scott, Walter, ed. and trans. *Hermetica.* 4 vols. 1924–1936. Reprint. London: Dawsons of Pall Mall, 1968.
Secret, François. *Les Kabbalistes chrétiens de la Renaissance.* Paris: Dunod, 1963.

Segal, Robert A. *The Poimandres as Myth: Scholarly Theory and Gnostic Meaning.* Vol. 33 of *Religion and Reason.* Berlin: Mouton de Gruyter, 1986.
Vickers, Brian, ed. *Occult and Scientific Mentalities in the Renaissance.* Cambridge: Cambridge University Press, 1984.
Walker, D. P. "The Astral Body in Renaissance Medicine." *Journal of the Warburg and Courtauld Institutes* 21 (1958): 119–33.
———. *Music, Spirit, and Language in the Renaissance.* Edited by Penelope Gouk. London: Variorum Reprints, 1985.
———. "Orpheus the Theologian and Renaissance Platonist." In *The Ancient Theology: Studies in Christian Platonism from the Fifteenth to the Eighteenth Century.* Ithaca: Cornell University Press, 1972.
———. *Spiritual and Demonic Magic from Ficino to Campanella.* 1958. Reprint. South Bend, Ind.: University of Notre Dame Press, 1975.
Wallis, R. T. *Neoplatonism.* London: Duckworth, 1972.
Westerink, L. G. *Texts and Studies in Neoplatonism and Byzantine Literature: Collected Papers.* Amsterdam: A. M. Hakkert, 1980.
Yates, Frances A. *Astraea: The Imperial Theme in the Sixteenth Century.* London: Routledge and Kegan Paul, 1975.
———. "Hermeticism." In *Encyclopedia of Philosophy.* New York: Macmillan, 1967.
———. "The Hermetic Tradition in Renaissance Science." In *Art, Science, and History in the Renaissance,* edited by C. S. Singleton. Baltimore: Johns Hopkins Press, 1967.
———. *The Occult Philosophy in the Elizabethan Age.* London: Routledge and Kegan Paul, 1979.
———. *The Rosicrucian Enlightenment.* London: Routledge and Kegan Paul, 1972.
———. *The Valois Tapestries.* London: Warburg Institute, University of London, 1959.
Zambelli, Paola. "Platone, Ficino, e la magia." In *Studia Humanitatis: Ernesto Grassi zum 70. Geburtstag,* edited by E. Hora and E. Kessler. Munich: W. Fink, 1973.

Prisca Theologia and Utopian Reform

This section contains relevant primary and secondary sources for Agrippa, Bruno, and Campanella; primary sources and interpretive studies for Bacon; and studies of the interrelation of science, religion, and utopias in the early modern period.

Agrippa, Bruno, and Campanella

Agrippa, Heinrich Cornelius. *Of the Vanitie and Uncertaintie of Artes and Sciences*. Edited by Catherine M. Dunn. Northridge, Calif.: California State University, 1974.

Bruno, Giordano. *The Ash Wednesday Supper*. Edited and translated by Edward A. Gosselin and Lawrence S. Lerner. Hamden, Conn.: Archon Books, 1977.

———. *The Expulsion of the Triumphant Beast*. Edited and translated by A. D. Imerti. New Brunswick, N.J.: Rutgers University Press, 1964.

Campanella, Tommaso. *The City of the Sun: A Poetical Dialogue*. Translated by Daniel J. Donno. Berkeley: University of California Press, 1981.

Nauert, Charles G., Jr. *Agrippa and the Crisis of Renaissance Thought*. Urbana: University of Illinois Press, 1965.

Nelson, John C. *Renaissance Theory of Love: The Context of Giordano Bruno's "Eroici furori."* New York: Columbia University Press, 1958.

Yates, Frances A. *Giordano Bruno and the Hermetic Tradition*. Chicago: University of Chicago Press, 1964.

———. *Lull and Bruno*. London: Routledge and Kegan Paul, 1982.

———. "The Religious Policy of Giordano Bruno." *Journal of the Warburg and Courtauld Institutes* 3 (1939–1940): 181–207.

Bacon

Bacon, Francis. *The Philosophical Works of Francis Bacon*. Edited by John M. Robertson. 1905. Reprint. Freeport, N.Y.: Books for Libraries Press, 1970.

———. *Works*. 14 vols. Edited by James Spedding, R. L. Ellis, and D. D. Heath. 1857–1874. Reprint. Stuttgart: Friedrich Fromann, 1963.

Lemmi, Charles W. *The Classic Deities in Bacon: A Study in Mythological Symbolism*. 1933. Reprint. New York: Octagon Books, 1971.

Linden, Stanton J. "Francis Bacon and Alchemy: The Reformation of Vulcan." *Journal of the History of Ideas* 35 (1974): 547–60.

Pérez-Ramos, Antonio. *Francis Bacon's Idea of Science and the Maker's Knowledge Tradition*. Oxford: Clarendon Press, 1988.

Rossi, Paolo. *Francis Bacon: From Magic to Science*. Translated by Sacha Rabinovitch. Chicago: University of Chicago Press, 1968.

———. "The New Science and the Symbol of Prometheus." In *Philosophy, Technology, and the Arts in the Early Modern Era*, translated by Salvator Attanasio and edited by Benjamin Nelson. New York: Harper and Row, 1970.

Weinberger, Jerry. *Science, Faith, and Politics: Francis Bacon and the Utopian Roots of the Modern Age*. Ithaca: Cornell University Press, 1985.
Whitney, Charles. *Francis Bacon and Modernity*. New Haven, Conn.: Yale University Press, 1986.

Religion, Science, and Utopianism

Ball, Brian W. *A Great Expectation: Eschatological Thought in English Protestantism to 1660*. Leiden: Brill, 1975.
Bauckham, Richard, ed. *Tudor Apocalypse: Sixteenth Century Apocalypticism, Millennarianism and the English Reformation*. . . . Oxford: Sutton Courtenay Press, 1978.
Christianson, Paul. *Reformers and Babylon: English Apocalyptic Visions from the Reformation to the Eve of the Civil War*. Toronto: University of Toronto Press, 1978.
Davis, J. C. *Utopia and the Ideal Society: A Study of English Utopian Writing, 1516-1700*. Cambridge: Cambridge University Press, 1981.
Debus, Allen G. *The Chemical Philosophy: Paracelsian Science and Medicine in the Sixteenth and Seventeenth Centuries*. 2 vols. New York: Science History Publications, 1977.
———. *Science and History: A Chemist's Appraisal*. Coimbra: Serviço de Documentaçao e Publicaçoes de Universidade de Coimbra, 1984.
Dobbs, Betty J. T. *The Foundations of Newton's Alchemy; or, "The Hunting of the Greene Lyon."* Cambridge: Cambridge University Press, 1975.
Dubos, Renée. *The Dreams of Reason: Science and Utopias*. New York: Columbia University Press, 1961.
Firth, Katharine R. *The Apocalyptic Tradition in Reformation Britain, 1530-1645*. Oxford: Oxford University Press, 1979.
Hill, Christopher. *The World Turned Upside Down: Radical Ideas During the English Revolution*. London: Temple Smith, 1972.
Jacob, James R. "Restoration, Reformation and the Origins of the Royal Society." *History of Science* 13 (1975): 155-76.
Jacob, James R., and Margaret C. Jacob. "The Anglican Origins of Modern Science: The Metaphysical Foundations of the Whig Constitution." *Isis* 71 (1980): 251-67.
Jacob, Margaret C. *The Newtonians and the English Revolution, 1689-1720*. Ithaca, N.Y.: Cornell University Press, 1976.
Jones, Richard F. *Ancients and Moderns: A Study of the Rise of the Scientific Movement in Seventeenth-Century England*. 2d ed. St. Louis: Washington University, 1961.
McGuire J. E., and P. M. Rattansi. "Newton and the 'Pipes of Pan.'" *Notes and Records of the Royal Society of London* 21 (1966): 108-43.

McKnight, Stephen A. "The Renaissance Magus and the Modern Messiah." *Religious Studies Review* 5 (1979): 81–89.

———. *Sacralizing the Secular: The Renaissance Origins of Modernity*. Baton Rouge, La.: Louisiana State University Press, 1989.

Olson, Theodore. *Millennialism, Utopianism, and Progress*. Toronto: University of Toronto Press, 1982.

Rattansi, P. M. "Paracelsus and the Puritan Revolution." *Ambix* 11 (1963): 24–32.

Reuther, Rosemary. *The Radical Kingdom: The Western Experience of Messianic Hope*. New York: Harper and Row, 1970.

Righini-Bonelli, M. L., and W. R. Shea, eds. *Reason, Experiment and Mysticism in the Scientific Revolution*. New York: Science History Publications, 1975.

Rossi, Paolo. *The Dark Abyss of Time: The History of the Earth and the History of Nations from Hooke to Vico*. Translated by Lydia G. Cochrane. Chicago: University of Chicago Press, 1984.

Sheppard, H. J. "A Survey of Alchemical and Hermetic Symbolism." *Ambix* 8 (February 1960): 35–41.

Thorndike, Lynn. *A History of Magic and Experimental Science*. 8 vols. New York: Macmillan, 1923–1958.

Walker, D. P. *The Ancient Theology: Studies in Christian Platonism from the Fifteenth to the Eighteenth Century*. Ithaca, N.Y.: Cornell University Press, 1972.

Webster, Charles. *From Paracelsus to Newton: Magic and the Making of Modern Science*. Cambridge: Cambridge University Press, 1982.

———. *The Great Instauration: Science, Medicine and Reform, 1642–1660*. New York: Holmes and Meier, 1976.

Westfall, Richard S. "Newton and the Hermetic Tradition." In *Science, Medicine and Society in the Renaissance*, edited by Allen G. Debus. New York: Science History Publications, 1972.

Westman, Robert S., and J. E. McGuire, eds. *Hermeticism and the Scientific Revolution: Papers Read at a Clark Library Seminar, March 9, 1974*. Los Angeles: William Andrews Clark Memorial Library, University of California, 1977.

Zilsel, Edgar. "The Genesis of the Concept of Scientific Progress." *Journal of the History of Ideas* 6 (1945): 325–49.

Index

Abraham, 65
Acheron, 84
Actio, 14
Actus purus, 11
Adam, 112, 113, 140
Adequatio: in hypothesis formation, 13-15
Adocentyn, 137
Aglophemus, 28
Agrippa, Heinrich Cornelius, 4, 26, 40, 41, 109-13, 118, 130, 141, 143; *De occulta philosophia,* 111, 112; *De incertitudine et vanitate scientiarum et artium,* 112
Alchemy, 1, 133, 138n11
Aleandro, Girolamo, Jr., 102-4
Alienation, 9, 15, 19, 23, 41, 99, 100, 110-12, 122, 142
Ancient Wisdom. See *Prisca theologia*
Anima mundi. See World soul
Anna (Wife of Joachim), 65, 67
Annunziata, Santa Maria, 64
Anthropos, 46. See also Terrestrial god
Apollo, 117
Apuleius, 107; *The Golden Ass,* 107, 108
Aquinas, Thomas, 18
Arena Chapel, 61, 64, 66, 73, 88, 91. See also Giotto; Scrovegni Chapel
Aristotle, 11, 16-18, 42; *Metaphysics,* 17
Asclepius, 27n2, 28, 34-36, 42, 48, 137. See also Ficino, Marsilio
Astral influences, 1, 4, 35, 42, 49, 50, 55, 60, 81, 93, 98, 106, 112, 122. See also Gods
Astrology, 49, 51, 78, 81, 106, 112
Athena, 93, 108. See also Gods; Minerva
Atlantis, 135, 141. See also Bacon, Francis: *New Atlantis*
Atlas, 27
Augustine, Saint, 3, 10, 14, 18,
Averroes, 18

Bacchus, 93, 101. See also Dionysus
Bacon, Francis, 2, 5, 15, 20, 26, 41, 109, 110, 126-33, 135-43; *Valerius terminus,* 20; *The Great Instauration (Instauratio magna),* 20, 127; *Novum Organum,* 20, 132; *New Atlantis,* 130-31, 133-36, 137, 140-42; *Advancement of Learning,* 130-33, 135n8, 140; "A Brief Discourse Touching the Happy Union of the Kingdoms of England and Scotland," 132-33; *De augmentis scientiarum,* 133; *Wisdom of the Ancients (De sapientia veterum),* 136, 141; "Prometheus or the State of Man," 137
Ben Salem, 133-36, 140, 141
Bethlehem, 68
Blumenberg, Hans, 3, 5, 14, 14n6, 15, 23, 24, 32, 36, 37, 42, 49, 60, 88, 89, 99, 109, 110, 115, 127, 128, 130, 141, 143, 144; *The Legitimacy of the Modern Age,* 2, 3, 6, 7n3, 24n12, 115n5; on secularization, 6-8; and Gnosticism, 8-9, 11-12, 23; and theodicy, 8-13, 40; description of epistemological transformation, 13, 16-20; analysis of curiosity, 16-20; legitimacy of modernity defended by, 21; in light of recent research 22, 25, 26, 28, 59; importance of Hermetic myth for, 30
Botticelli, Sandro, 4, 77, 82, 90-93, 95, 96, 98, 102-4, 106, 108; *Minerva and the Centaur,* 4, 91, 92, 93-95, 101, 108; *The Birth of Venus,* 4, 91, 92, 95-96, 101; *La Primavera,* 4, 91, 96-97, 101-3, 108
Bruno, Giordano, 4, 5, 40, 41, 113-22, 131, 136, 141; *The Ash Wednesday Supper (Cena de le ceneri),* 114, 115, 116-20; *The Expulsion of the Triumphant Beast (Spaccio della bestia trionfante),* 120; *Purgatorio de l'inferno,* 120

157

Burckhardt, Jakob, 25
Byzantine, 27, 60, 61, 71, 73

Cabala, 1, 111, 112, 134
Calabria, 122, 123, 125
Campanella, Tomasso, 4, 5, 109, 122–26, 130, 141; *The City of the Sun (La Città del Sole)*, 122, 123, 125, 126; *Monarchia di Spagna*, 124; *Monarchia Messiae*, 124; *Eclogue*, 125
Catholic League, 121
Centaur, 91–94, 101, 102, 108
Chaldeans, 57, 118
Chiron, 94
Chloris, 102–4
Christ, 61, 65, 71, 73, 76, 87, 112, 123, 124, 133, 134
Christianity, 1–4, 14, 32, 134, 143; and secularization, 6–8; and Gnosticism, 8–10; and medieval theology, 10–13, 18–26; and Renaissance art, 60–90 *passim*; and Hermetic reform, 110–24 *passim*
Chronos, 95
Cicero, 16
Cocytus, 84
College of Solomon, 135*n*9
College of the Six Days Works, 135
Columbus, Christopher, 116
Copernicus, Nicolaus, 5, 114–17, 119; Copernicanism, 113–15
Corpus Hermeticum, 23*n*11, 27, 28, 98, 100, 101, 130
Cosmology, 8, 19, 21, 23, 24, 49, 84, 93, 111, 115, 120
Council of Florence, 27
Cox-Rearick, Janet, 78
Crucifixion, 65
Cupid, 97, 98, 101, 105
Curiosity, 16–21, 24, 99, 107, 108; *Curiositas*, 16, 19, 99
Cynics, 16

Dante, 20; *Divine Comedy*, 64*n*2
Debus, Allen G., 26*n*13
Demiurge, 17, 32, 36; in Gnosticism, 8–10; in theological absolutism, 13–14; in Hermetic myth, 29, 30
Democritus, 139

Dempsey, Charles, 92, 98, 99, 102–7
Descartes, René, 13
Desire, 20, 48, 53, 95, 97, 113. *See also* Love; Passion
Deus absconditus, 2, 19
Dionysus, 101. *See also* Bacchus
Divine intellect, 34, 52
Dixon, John W., Jr., 85, 87
Dobbs, B. J. T., 26*n*13
Duccio, 61, 64, 73; *Rucellai Madonna*, 61, 62

Eden, 18, 37
Egypt, 36, 71, 134, 137; in Gnostic myth, 38; Egyptians, 38, 39, 57, 118; Egyptian religion, 122. *See also* Hermeticism
Elizabeth I (queen of England), 121
Empedocles, 139
Epicureanism, 18
Epimetheus, 137, 140
Epochal phases, 1, 2, 6–8, 12, 22, 23, 25, 28, 42, 88, 109, 110, 115, 127, 128, 142, 143
Eschatology, 7, 8
Eschaton, 7
Eucharist: described by Bruno, 119
Eudoxus, 117
Evil, 8–10, 14, 32, 33, 36, 40, 55, 88, 138

Fate, 29, 31, 34, 44, 52, 57, 106–8, 110, 112, 125, 128
Favonius, 102, 103. *See also* Zephyr winds
Ficino, Marsilio, 1–4, 24, 26–27, 32, 34, 44*n*3, 53*n*17, 78, 81, 82, 96, 98, 100, 106–8, 110–12, 122, 126, 131, 136, 139, 143; role of *prisca theologia* in work of, 22–23, 28, 36, 40–61 *passim*, 89–95; and new understanding of human nature, 22–23, 42–59 *passim*, 94–95, 101–2; genealogy of Hermes by, 28; on magic, 40, 49–58, 106–7; on the soul, 43, 52–57, 77, 94–95, 101–2; discussion of world soul by, 51–54; on *spiritus*, 51–54; and talismans, 55–58
—Works: *Pimander*, 28–34, 36, 40, 42, 48, 98, 100, 101, 111; *Theologia Pla-*

tonica, 4, 28, 42–49, 50–60, 94, 110; *De Christiana Religione*, 42; *De vita triplici*, 42, 49–59 *passim*, 94, 106, 110, 139; *De triplici ratione cognoscendi Deum*, 110, 112
Flora, 97, 102–4
Florence, 4, 91
Fowden, Garth, 98–101, 108
Freedom, 10, 11, 13, 14, 18, 44, 88, 129

Galileo, 5, 19, 114; *Dialogue Concerning the Two Chief World Systems*, 114
Garin, Eugenio, 24, 40
Genesis, 36, 37, 111
Giotto, 4, 60, 61, 64–73 *passim*, 76, 88, 89, 91
—Works: *The Ognissanti Madonna*, 61, 63; *The Annunciation of the Virgin*, 65, 71; *The Last Judgment*, 65, 76; *Joachim's Expulsion from the Temple*, 67; *Joachim's Return to the Shepherds*, 68; *The Dream of Joachim*, 69; *The Sacrifice of Joachim*, 69; *The Meeting at the Golden Gate*, 70; *Prologue in Heaven*, 70, 76; *The Anunciation of the Virgin*, 71; *The Wedding Feast at Cana*, 71, 72; *The Adoration of the Magi*, 72; *The Resurrection of Lazarus*, 73, 74; *The Lamentation*, 73, 74. *See also* Arena Chapel
Gnosis, 39, 99
Gnosticism, 3, 14, 15, 28, 30, 32n6, 37, 39, 88, 99, 108, 109; cosmology of, 8–12; curiosity in, 18; in Blumenberg's thought, 23; self-assertion of, 40
God, 1, 2–3, 7–9, 18, 20, 23–25, 39, 40, 43–49, 55, 58–61, 65, 73, 76–82 *passim*, 85, 89, 92, 95, 96, 100, 102, 111, 113, 116, 119, 125, 126, 129, 130, 135, 143; and theodicy, 8–10, 88; as absolute, 10–13, 14, 21; and revelation, 19, 28, 34, 36, 87, 93, 94, 101, 108–10, 112, 134; in Hermetic myth, 29–37
Gods, 18, 28, 34–36, 57, 82, 98, 121, 128, 138, 139. *See also* Apollo; Athena; Bacchus; Chronos; Dionysus; Jove; Jupiter; Hermes; Mars; Mercury; Minerva; Saturn; Vulcan; Zeus

Gombrich, E. H., 91, 93, 102, 105, 107
Gosselin, Edward A., 113, 114n3
Governors: in Hermetic myth, 29–31. *See also* Astral influences
Graces, 97, 98, 101, 105, 107

Hades, 84
Heilsgeschichte, 7, 14n6, 21
Héliaca, 125. *See also* Campanella, Tomasso: *City of the Sun*
Henry of Navarre, 121
Henry III (king of France), 121
Heraclitus, 132
Hercules, 138. *See also* Pillars of Hercules
Hermes, 28, 33; in *Minerva and the Centaur*, 93. *See also* Mercury
Hermes Trismegistus, 28n4, 31, 32, 36, 37, 47, 58; Ficino's genealogy, 27; revelatory experience in *Asclepius*, 34, 36; compared to James I, 131–33
Hermeticism, 1, 3, 4, 23n9, 27n2, 36, 37n16, 49, 50, 59, 77, 79–85 *passim*, 108, 110, 112, 115, 118, 122, 124, 126, 142; man as a terrestrial god in, 24; impact on Christianity of, 26; compared to Blumenberg's concept of Gnosticism, 37; and Gnosticism, 37–40; and inner-worldly fulfillment, 40; *paideia*, 91–94, 98–102, 105–6
Historical consciousness, 6, 14
Holy Family, 65
Homonoia (like-mindedness), 35n12, 100
Horae, 105
House of Solomon, 130, 134, 140. *See also* College of the Six Days Works; College of Solomon
Human nature, 2, 3, 10n4, 13, 21, 28, 41, 47, 50, 59, 71, 89, 90, 92, 99, 100, 101, 110, 111, 139, 143, 144; and self-assertion, 6, 9, 11–15, 21, 22, 24, 40, 42, 115; in Gnosticism, 9–10, 39–40; modern transformation of, 13–22 *passim*; in Ficino, 22–23, 42–59 *passim*, 94–95, 101–2; in Hermetic myth, 29–37 *passim*
"Hymn of the Pearl," 37–39. *See also* Gnosticism

Immanentism, 12, 23, 60, 76, 77, 89, 91
Incarnation, 76, 95–96, 98
Inquisition, 113
Inspiration, 92, 101, 105, 107. *See also* Revelation
Intellect, 34, 35, 44, 51–54, 56, 58, 82, 85, 138. *See also* Mind; *Mens*

Jaeger, Werner, 99
James I (king of England), 128, 129, 131, 140–42
Jerusalem, 73, 79. *See also* Jerusalem, New
Jerusalem, New, 129, 137, 142. *See also* Bacon, Francis: *New Atlantis*
Jesus, 71, 73
Joachim, 65, 67
John the Baptist, 5, 115
Joseph, 65, 67
Josiah, 129
Jove, 93, 95. *See also* Astral influences; Gods; Jupiter; Zeus
Julius II, 78, 79, 87
Jupiter, 52, 56, 81, 107, 123, 137–39. *See also* Astral influences; Gods; Jove; Zeus

Klibansky, R., *See Saturn and Melancholy*

Landino, Francesco, 78
Leo X, 78
Lightbown, Ronald, 92
Logos, 30, 33*n*7, 37, 39; role in Hermetic myth, 33
Louis XIII (king of France), 123
Louis XIV (king of France), 125, 126
Love, 24, 31, 32, 33*n*8, 38, 44, 67, 76, 77, 88, 89, 92, 95–101 *passim,* 106, 124, 125, 136, 140. *See also* Desire
Löwith, Karl, 6, 7, 128
Lucretius, 104
Luther, Martin, 113

Macrocosm, 24, 37, 42, 60, 61, 78, 81, 82, 88, 119
Magi, 1, 28, 68, 118, 124, 132, 133
Magic, 24, 35, 49, 50, 58, 59, 77, 91, 93, 98, 110, 112, 122, 124, 125, 126, 133, 136, 141

Magician, 50, 58, 90, 111, 128, 141
Magnum miraculum, 35
Magus, 32, 37, 40, 49, 50, 57–59, 110, 111, 121, 126, 130, 131, 134, 141, 142
Marcion, 9, 37*n*16
Mars, 81, 107. *See also* Astral influences; Gods
Mary, 65, 67, 68
Matthew: Michelangelo's sculpture of, 87
Medici Chapel, 60, 76–79, 82, 84–89, 91; interior, 80; cupola, 79, 81; tomb of Lorenzo de'Medici, 83; tomb of Giuliano de'Medici, 83; Medici Virgin and Child, 86
Medici family, 22, 27, 82, 103; Tomb of Cosimo, 78; Giuliano, 78, 88; Lorenzo, 78, 88, 93; Lorenzino, 91–93, 101, 106, 108. *See also* Ficino, Marsilio; Michelangelo
Melancholy 49–51, 84, 94
Mens, 28, 29. *See also* Mind
Mentalité, 77
Mercury, 81, 93, 97, 98, 101–7, 117, 123; in Minerva and the Centaur, 93. *See also* Astral influences; Gods
Messiah, 112, 121
Messianic, 93, 114, 115, 122, 125
Michelangelo, 4, 60, 61, 76–79, 82, 84, 85, 87–91, 106. *See also* Medici Chapel
Microcosm, 24, 39, 42, 47, 78, 81, 88, 119
Middle Ages, 2, 3, 6, 7, 15, 23, 24, 40, 49, 61, 64, 73, 79, 82, 88, 109, 144; as an epochal phase, 12; theological absolutism in, 21
Mind, 28–30, 32, 44, 47, 48, 51–54, 56-58, 89, 93, 95, 100, 105, 117, 118, 121, 132, 138, 139. *See also* Intellect; *Mens; Nous*
Minerva, 51, 91–93, 95, 101, 108, 138, 140. *See also* Athena; Gods
Modern age, illegitimacy of, 7–8
Modernity, 2, 5, 6–9, 12–16, 19–26, 28, 40–42, 49, 50, 59, 65, 88, 89, 109, 110, 113–18 *passim,* 128, 129, 141, 142, 143
Mohammed, 123

Index

Moon, 57, 81, 103, 125. *See also* Astral influences
Moses, 27, 36, 87, 123, 129, 134
Muses, 51
Myth, 8, 16–18, 28, 30, 32, 33, 37, 39, 95, 109, 115, 130, 137, 141

Neoplatonic School in Alexandria, 22
Neoplatonism, 1, 4, 43, 50, 59, 60, 76, 91–92, 94, 98, 106, 108, 143; role in Ancient Wisdom of, 22; revival of, 26; in Renaissance art, 77–90; and cosmology, 79–85
Newton, Isaac, 26
Nolan. *See* Bruno, Giordano
Nominalism, 2, 3, 6, 9–12, 14, 25, 26, 89, 144; theological absolutism of, 12, 14, 21; curiosity in, 19
Nous, 29–31, 33, 34, 37, 100, 105. *See also* Intellect; *Mens*; Mind

Odysseus, 20
Old Testament, 9, 10, 65, 87
Orpheus, 28, 48, 118, 136, 141
Osiris, 123
Ovid, 104, 107

Padua, 4, 60, 61, 64
Paideia, 91, 93, 98–102, 105, 106, 108
Pandora, 137, 139
Panofsky, Erwin, 49, 77, 84–88 *passim*. *See also* Saturn and Melancholy
Paris, judgment of, 107
Parousia, 9
Parthenon, 93
Passion, 93, 95, 98. *See also* Desire; Love
Paul's Epistle to the Romans, 10
Perfect society, 40, 41, 99, 100, 113, 126. *See also* Utopia
Peripatetics, 139
Persians: Bacon's discussion of magi-king, 132
Philolaus, 28
Philosophes, 7
Phlegethon, 84
Pico della Mirandola, Giovanni, 40, 110–12
Pillars of Hercules, 15, 20, 21, 127
Plato, 17, 23, 27, 28, 135; cosmology of, 8; curiosity in writings of, 16; *Phaedo*, 16; *Timaeus*, 16; role in *Theologia Platonica*, 22, 42; *Symposium*, 42, 95
Platonic Academy, 2, 4, 22, 60, 61, 77, 78, 91; establishment of, 27
Platonists, 47; and planetary influences, 57
Pletho, Gemistus, 27
Plotinus, 27; *Commentaries*, 28n4; in the *De vita*, 58
Plutarch, 103
Political reform, 122, 129. *See also* Perfect society; Utopia
Poliziano, Angelo, 78, 92; *Rusticus*, 103
Pontormo, Jacopo da, 78
Pre-Socratics, 16
Prima materia, 32, 82
Prisca theologia (Ancient Wisdom), 1, 3–5, 20, 22, 23n10, 24–28, 40–41, 42, 50, 52, 55, 59–60, 77, 109, 111, 114–16, 120, 122, 128, 130–31, 141, 142, 143; in recent research, 22–26; and Platonic Academy, 60–61, 91; and modern age, 109, 111–12, 114, 116; in Agrippa, 111–13; in Bruno, 114–18; in Bacon, 127–37.
Progress, 6, 7, 21, 22, 24–35, 40, 59, 108, 117, 127
Prometheus, 27, 137–41
Psychomachia, 77
Pythagoras, 27n1
Pythagoreans, 28, 50, 118

Redemption, 9, 11, 101, 120. *See also* Salvation
Renaissance, 1, 3, 4, 22, 23, 25, 27, 46, 49, 50, 59–61, 64, 73, 76–78, 81, 84, 88, 89–92, 94, 109, 110, 141, 143
Resurrection, 7, 65, 68, 73, 82, 87
Revelation, 19, 36, 87, 93, 94, 101, 108–10, 112, 122, 134; in Hermeticism, 27–35. *See also* Inspiration
Richelieu, Cardinal, 123
Rosicrucian, 142
Royal Society of London, 127

Saeculum, 7, 8
Salvation, 7, 9–12, 18–21, 32, 33, 37,

39, 40, 64, 77, 87, 88, 100, 108, 109, 130, 134. *See also* Redemption
Salvation history, 7. *See also Heilsgeschichte*
San Lorenzo, 61, 78
Sarah, 65
Sarbûg: in Gnostic myth, 38
Saturn, 49, 50, 56, 81, 107. *See also* Astral influences; Gods
Saturn and Melancholy (Klibanski, Panofsky, Saxl): discussion of human dignity in, 49; human mastery of nature in, 50, 59
Saxl, F., *See Saturn and Melancholy*
Scardeone, Bernardino, 64
Scholasticism, 2, 88, 89, 108, 110, 113, 144; cosmos of, 10–12; curiosity in, 18–19
Science, 19, 20, 24–26, 49, 54, 59, 96, 113–15, 127, 132, 133, 141, 143
Scientific Revolution, 25, 110
Scrovegni, Enrico, 60, 64
Scrovegni, Reginaldo, 64
Scrovegni Chapel, 4
Secularization, 6–9, 14n6, 143
Self-assertion, 6, 9, 11–15, 21, 22, 24, 40, 42, 115
Seznec, Jean, 91
Sin, 10, 18, 20, 31–33, 36, 37, 65, 88, 89, 112, 113, 128, 130, 142
Skepticism, 18
Socrates, 16, 17
Solomon, 129–31, 134, 135, 140–42
Sophism, 16
Soul, 9, 16, 17, 33, 39, 42–44, 46–48, 50–54, 56–58, 60, 61, 77–79, 82, 84, 85, 87–89, 91, 94, 95, 97, 98, 101, 105, 110, 113
Spiritus mundi. *See* World spirit
Stoicism, 18
Styx, 84
Sun, 56

Talismans, 35, 50, 55, 98, 99. *See also* Astral influences; Magic
Temple of Solomon, 129, 130, 141
Terrestrial god: man as, 4, 23–25, 44, 46, 49, 59, 111–13, 126
Theodicy, 2, 8, 10, 15, 88
Tiphys, 116
Tolnay, Charles de, 79, 82, 85–87
Toth, 98
Tower of Babel, 37
Tree of Knowledge, 37
Tree of Life, 37
Trismegistus. *See* Hermes Trismegistus

Uranos, 95
Urban VIII, 122, 125, 126
Utopia, 7, 109, 122, 123, 125–27, 130, 133, 137, 143. *See also* Perfect society; Political reform

Vasari, Giorgio, 77, 91
Venus, 52, 81, 91–93, 95, 96, 97, 98, 101–8; in Botticelli's *Minerva and the Centaur*, 93. *See also* Astral influences
Vespucci family, 93
Villa di Castello, 91, 103
Virgil: *Aeneid*, 94; *Fourth Eclogue*, 125
Voltaire, 7
Vulcan, 137

Walker, D. P., 22, 49, 50
Wallace, Robert M., 12–13.
Whitney, Charles, 128, 142
Wind, Edgar, 91, 105
World soul (*anima mundi*), 17, 42, 52–54, 58
World spirit (*spiritus mundi*), 35, 42, 51, 53, 54, 58.

Xenophon, 16

Yates, Frances, 24, 33n8, 114, 121–24

Zephyr winds, 95, 96, 97, 102–4
Zeus, 101. *See also* Astral influences; Gods; Jove; Jupiter
Zoroaster, 28n4